"Young women are desperate for men~~~~~~elationships that help heal their brokenness. *Organic Mentoring* sheds light on why traditional methods flounder and offers fresh, insightful, and useful suggestions to meet the challenges of mentoring next generation women. This book shows us how to pass on our faith while moving from print to technology in relationships and life."

—**Elisa Morgan,** speaker, author, *The Beauty of Broken,* publisher, *FullFill,* and president emerita of MOPS International

"When I've asked Christian women what they feel they need most of all to thrive as a Christian and survive as a leader, one of the most common answers is 'a mentor.' Without mentors, women constantly have to recreate the wheel because they don't have the benefit of hearing the wise counsel of one who has tread their path before. The trouble is that the generational differences between older and younger women are vast and they prohibit these types of relationships from developing. In their book, *Organic Mentoring,* Sue Edwards and Barbara Neumann address these differences and build a bridge across that generational divide. If you're an older woman who has longed to impart the wisdom you've gleaned from the years but weren't sure how to go about it, get this book! Sue and Barbara have provided a guide that will help you navigate the mentoring relationship with aplomb."

—**Halee Gray Scott**, author of *Dare Mighty Things: Mapping the Challenges of Leadership for Christian Women*

"I love this book! I will definitely incorporate it into several contexts, including my seminary classroom teaching as well as personal relationships. Generational differences have clearly stalled the mentoring advantage. *Organic Mentoring* gets us moving again in a world that desperately needs the benefit of intergenerational mentoring. The text provides valuable understanding, plus practical tips and tools offered to leaders, mentors, and mentees. This useful resource will inevitably stimulate healthy, organic relationships with next generation women!"

—**Bev Hislop**, Professor of Pastoral Care, Western Seminary, and author of *Shepherding a Woman's Heart* and *Shepherding Women in Pain*

"I am a product of mentoring. It changed my life, my family, and my future. The spiritual investment other women made in my life changed the course of history. In God's Word there are only a few times where the Lord asks women to do a specific thing for him and mentoring is one of them. He doesn't say how exactly, but the command is clear, not optional. Thankfully, Sue Edwards and Barbara Neumann tell us how, and outline some specifics for successfully mentoring the next generation. They provide a new "mentoring mind-set" with a fresh approach that feels natural and meaningful, and results in something supernatural. Speaking truth into the life of a younger woman doesn't require a program, it requires authenticity, connection, and understanding the needs of the younger woman. *Organic Mentoring* is the resource every woman needs to accomplish the assignment the Lord has given us. As a former director of women's ministry for twenty years, I have seen and experienced the struggles with trying to make a mentoring ministry work, and I am so excited about this resource that explains, instructs, and encourages organic mentoring."

—**Debbie Stuart**, Church and Leadership Development Director for Women of Faith, and former director of women's ministry at Prestonwood Baptist Church

"*Organic Mentoring* offers crucial insights toward the relational work of the Great Commission in our current generations—mentoring, discipling, teaching, and training. By thoughtfully and practically describing both the disconnects and the common desires between modern and postmodern generations, this book gives us needed clarity to restore vital guiding relationships in this age of technology. The authors ignite our hope to recapture the vanishing blessing of the transforming relationships that help us connect life and truth!"

—**Wendy Wilson**, Consultant for Ministry Development of Women, Missio Nexus —Professional Services Group

"Sue Edwards and Barbara Neumann have given evangelical women an extraordinary gift in their new book, *Organic Mentoring*. With accurate data, keen cultural insights, and a solid biblical foundation, they give us a fresh understanding of how to effectively mentor the next generation. The section on training will help sharpen leaders' skills and rekindle their vision for developing meaningful relationships among women. Timely and practical, this book will encourage you to take mentoring to the next level and beyond!"

—**Susie Hawkins**, Bible teacher and author of *From One Ministry Wife to Another*

"We live in a world of Instagram, Twitter, and Facebook, where the goal of a conversation is to pass along information in as little time, with as little small talk, as possible. Yet the heart cry is still the same—*walk with me through this complicated journey called life*. Sue and Barbara unwrap and untangle the differing aspects of our generations, help us to understand and respect each other, and thus awaken a desire to pass truth along to the next generation. But they don't stop with understanding and respect, *Organic Mentoring* sets forth the how-to and the why—the practical tools needed to embark on, and enjoy, this journey with one another. *Organic Mentoring* will take a prominent place on my bookshelf and in my ministry as I, and others, strive to transform lives and grow his kingdom."

—**Cynthia Fantasia**, Pastor, Service and Women, Grace Chapel

"As a ministry leader, I will be recommending this well-written and engaging book frequently. In fact, I'm just going to keep it in stock. Questions about mentoring come up all the time. And every woman who desires to be in a mentoring relationship needs to read this book! It is long overdue. Sue and Barbara have expressed what my heart knew to be true about mentoring. You see, I am a postmodern woman and a casualty of formal mentoring programs. But I'm not ready to give up on mentoring; it's biblical, it's necessary, and women desire it. This book is the tool I have been looking for. It corrects mistaken thinking and encourages modern women to move toward a way of mentorship that postmodern women long for. I can't wait to get this into the hands of my leadership team!"

—**Jodie Niznik**, Pastor to Women, Irving Bible Church

Organic
MENTORING

A MENTOR'S GUIDE TO RELATIONSHIPS
WITH NEXT GENERATION WOMEN

SUE EDWARDS & BARBARA NEUMANN

Kregel
Ministry

Organic Mentoring: A Mentor's Guide to Relationships with Next Generation Women

© 2014 by Sue Edwards and Barbara Neumann

Published by Kregel Publications, a division of Kregel, Inc., 2450 Oak Industrial Dr. NE, Grand Rapids, MI 49505-6020.

ISBN 978-0-8254-4333-6

Printed in the United States of America

14 15 16 17 18 / 5 4 3 2 1

To our mentors:
You poured into two lonely, misguided young women
with little to offer, and God used you to completely change
the direction of our lives.

To our mentees:
You gave us opportunity to pass on the beautiful gifts
we received from others and to redeem our broken lives
for the glory of God.
Pass it on, dear ones, pass it on!

Contents

Acknowledgments

In normal life we hardly realize how much more we receive than we give, and life cannot be rich without such gratitude. It is so easy to overestimate the importance of our own achievements compared with what we owe to the help of others.

Dietrich Bonhoeffer,
Letters and Papers from Prison

We owe a debt of gratitude to an army of fellow professors and students, authors and leaders, family and friends, who supported us in our quest to better understand mentoring today and to write a resource that we believe will strengthen mentoring relationships. We live in unsettling times of extreme transition. Our seminary students sometimes ask, "How should ministry change in response to the tsunami of transitions evident today? What does God want us to do?" This book was written in response to those kinds of questions and with gratitude for many insightful conversations with young students that influenced this work. Our fervent hope is that *Organic Mentoring* will help mentors navigate the mentoring crisis we are experiencing today and, as a result, multitudes of older and younger women will find relational havens that help them both gain their bearings and stand strong in shifting times.

Thanks is due to particular people who aided us with this project. First, to Sheryl Lackey, Sue's seminary intern, who secured the next generation responses found at the end of each chapter. They add depth and credibility to our ideas. She also sat through long hours of editing sessions, read-throughs, laughter, and nibbling, contributing valuable insights reflecting her understanding and heart for younger women. The book is better for your input. Thanks, Sheryl.

Thanks to the group of outstanding young women who prompted Barbara's research. Over the years we gathered in various living rooms to explore thoughts, questions, struggles, and insights into godly living amidst the challenges of the twenty-first century. Lisa, Shanna, Kathryn, Sarah, Jocelyn, Carol, Holly, Carrie, Kelly, Susan, Kim, Missy, Liz, and Meagan—your preferences, disappointments, and dreams permeate these pages.

And thanks to our beautiful daughters, Heather Edwards Crook, Rachel Edwards Boone, Jessica Neumann Joslin, Kristin Sanderson Neumann, and Juliet Neumann Purvis, who show us daily just how interesting, gifted, and precious young women are. You mentored us in the art of mentoring.

And behind every married female author is a supportive husband, and ours deserve more than we could ever repay. Thanks David and Ralph for the evenings and weekends you spent alone so we could brainstorm and wordsmith. Your personal sacrifices made the birth of this book possible.

We also appreciate the great team at Kregel Publications. We've worked together for over a decade, and you've exhibited constant integrity, professionalism, expertise, and Christlike character. No wonder you've been around since 1949! Thanks for the partnership and opportunity to influence people through top quality resources.

Finally, all praise and thanksgiving to God Almighty in the Persons of the Glorious Father, Gracious Son, and Powerful Holy Spirit. May whatever good comes out of the labor of love on these pages go to your honor and glory. Amen.

Part I

Why Something New?

Barbara's Story

I vividly remember a time when I desperately needed someone to show the way. I was driving through the Texas panhandle headed north to Colorado. It was night and a wintry storm was visible on weather radar, but it appeared light and I wasn't too concerned. This would be a good time to mention that I am a south Texas girl who knows nothing about winter storms on radar, hence the foolish decision to keep going.

Once I was well into the middle of nowhere, the light snow turned into a nasty blizzard. Ice caked on my windshield wipers, rendering them useless. The fierce north Texas wind blew snow across the highway, and eventually the road disappeared. I began to panic as I realized I couldn't continue forward or turn back, and the darkness revealed no headlights in either direction for many miles. I was alone.

My trusty companion, my cell phone, showed no bars. I prayed out loud. Prayer accelerated to fearful pleading as I inched along an imaginary highway. I will never forget the overwhelming relief that washed over me when I made out two red taillights ahead. I was not alone on this road after all! I caught up to an eighteen-wheeler expertly navigating the treacherous highway in front of me. God mercifully gave me an experienced driver to follow to the next sign of civilization where I pulled off the highway and waited out the storm in an eight-room motel. I have blessed eighteen-wheeler drivers ever since.

I can look back to my days as a young woman and see times that a mentor could have made a huge difference in my life. I was raised in a non-Christian, alcoholic home, and was traveling alone on an invisible highway. Although I came to faith in Jesus at age twenty-two, I was still confused about life and had no one to guide me to solid ground. I yearned to be a strong woman of God, but questions outweighed answers. Who is God? What does He require? How should I think or act in this situation? Available Bible teaching, though sound and insightful, came forth from male voices and perspectives. How do I live my life as a woman devoted to Christ? Many young women continue to ask these questions and seek an experienced guide to show the way. Mentoring is a primary way God provides direction for the young women He deeply loves.

Sue's Story

Like Barbara, I was raised in a non-Christian home, deeply wounded by a dysfunctional mother, scarred, and on the road to disaster, when Jesus rescued me at age twenty-four. I too remember the red taillights ahead that led me to new life in Christ. A neighbor invited me to a women's Bible study and for the next fifteen years, God used women there to heal me. Was it mentoring, re-mothering, coaching, lay counseling, encouraging, advising, or training? Whatever you call it, these terms picture nuances of a powerful relationship between two women as they influence one another to wholeheartedly seek God and fully grow up in Him.

C. S. Lewis captured the essence of this relationship from the older person's perspective when he said, "Think of me as a fellow patient in the same hospital, who having been admitted a little earlier, could give some advice."[1] Those women surrounded me with their love. We did life together, and, yes, they gave me great advice. God used their influence to heal my heart and mind, to nurture a dynamic relationship with Almighty God, to resurrect a broken marriage, to transform my mothering, and to train me with skills that help me today as I teach and mentor, along with Barbara, in a major seminary and in our local churches.

Ditch Worn-Out Mentoring Models

We are experiencing a mentoring crisis today. One key reason is that too many of us older women cling to an outdated formulaic idea of what

---

1   C. S. Lewis, "Letter to Sheldon Vanauken of 22nd April 1953," in *A Severe Mercy*, Sheldon Vanauken (San Francisco: Harper Collins, 1977), 134.

mentoring is all about. When we hear the word *mentoring,* we conjure up a picture that fits our experience as young women. Then we look in the mirror and don't see an adequate mentor staring back at us. Our preconceived ideas about what today's young women want in a mentor convince us we are not enough—but we are wrong. What we don't realize is that younger women today are far more likely to want a relationship with the woman in the mirror than the conjured-up perfect mentor in our heads.

Or we think about our busy lives and determine that we just don't have the time to invest in younger women's lives. That's because we envision a tight, often weekly commitment level, and we cringe. What we don't realize is that younger women cringe too. Most don't want, nor will they allocate, that many hours out of their busy lives either.

Or we assume that we must step into the role of Bible-answer-woman. We think that we will need to prepare lessons from a formal Bible curriculum and teach our charges essentials of the faith—like how to share their testimony or how to memorize Scripture. We don't realize that most young women today are not looking for a Bible-answer-woman. Instead, they want an honest woman with whom they can process life.

Our excuses for not mentoring are based on preconceptions that just aren't true anymore. Young women don't want what older women think they want. And the excuses that flood our minds when we hesitate to take on a mentoring relationship aren't valid today. Sadly, our ideas about mentoring keep us from stepping into young women's lives, leaving too many young women alone on those invisible highways.

Our Flagship Text

We find the answer to our mentoring crisis in God's Word. After leading the Israelites out of slavery in Egypt and into the Promised Land. Moses wrote,

> Love the LORD your God with all your heart and with all your soul and with all your strength. These commandments that I give you today are to be on your hearts. Impress them on your children. Talk about them when you sit at home and when you walk along the road, when you lie down and when you get up. (Deuteronomy 6:5–7)

Moses first wrote these words for parents to help them pass on their faith to their children, but they apply equally well to us as mentors mandated to guide our spiritual children on those invisible highways. Moses instructs us to "impress" (*Shanan*) our love for God on our mentees, but to do so in a natural kind of way. The Hebrew word for impress means to whet their appetites for God, to sharpen them spiritually. He tells us to mentor *when you sit at home and when you walk along the road, when you lie down and when you get up.* These verses ooze a casual, natural informality.

Moses asked parents to speak of their love for God in those natural everyday moments of life, sitting together at home, walking from place to place, to take advantage of teachable times when questions naturally arise. We adapt this concept to mentoring when our relationships take on an informal feel, simply doing life together. We call this new approach to mentoring *organic*, and we'll unpack the term and how it applies to mentoring throughout the book. What a surprise to find our answer to the mentoring crisis in ancient biblical wisdom.

Generational Slander

If you write a book, interested friends often ask what it's about and how your work is progressing. My (Sue) home group was enjoying dinner one night, and as we sat around the table, one of the men initiated a conversation about our book by asking those kinds of questions. Talking about your book is a bit like talking about your grandchildren; you welcome their interest and enjoy answering. Soon we were talking about young people, and unfortunately the conversation deteriorated into an exuberant game of "ain't it awful."

More has changed in the last fifty years than in the last five hundred years, resulting in a tsunami of required adjustments, particularly by older generations. The Judeo-Christian ethic that permeated the ethos of the Western world has dried up, and the resulting demise of moral standards and the escalation of bad behavior sends many older folks reeling. Christians in my home group work hard to remain positive in the midst of what many perceive as political and economic chaos, but seething attitudes often simmer just beneath the surface.

Our discussion that evening about helping young people triggered explosive comments from several of my dear friends. Comments like "Why should we have to adjust to them? They are the ones causing the problems," and "It's at times like this that I just figure God will save the people He wants to save." A subtle way of saying "Let's just let them go to hell." Raw words spew out of the mouths of mature Christians who know the Bible and love the Lord but are incredibly frustrated with the corruption and collapse of what they hold dear.

Disheartened and perplexed, many of our peers blame young people, understandable but counterproductive. We struggle too, but venting, criticizing, and generational slander won't honor the name of Christ, bring glory to God, or help us connect with younger generations.

A New Approach Deserves a New Label

Here it is. We propose no label at all. The word *mentoring* conjures up so many stereotypes and hang-ups that we prefer to stop using it or any formal word for the relationship. That's a more organic approach and may help us older women rid ourselves of expectations that tend to discourage us from "mentoring" anyway.

We enjoy sweet relationships with a number of women in our seminary and in our churches, but they seldom begin with a formal invitation like "Will you be my mentor?" It just happens, and later that woman will intro-duce us to someone as her "mentor," which is fine, but we are always a bit jarred by the term. The old tapes in our heads cause us to frown and ask, "Am I doing all I should be doing as her mentor?" And we have to stop and rethink what it means to be those taillights on that invisible road. We have to remember that our traditional mentoring picture is not her mentoring picture. Then we can breathe again and our relationship continues in a natural way that actually works better for us all.

We'll use the terms *organic mentoring, mentor,* and *mentee* in this book because we need to call it something. But we encourage you to move away from formal terms as a first step in adopting a new mentoring mind-set, and we'll give you plenty of reasons why in the pages ahead.

Why We Wrote This Book

Our passion is to help you understand, feed, and grow other women in the Lord, in light of the massive shift in the perspectives and attitudes of younger women today. As we said, the ways we were mentored simply do not work with this new female breed. From our own experiences, from concerns peers have voiced, and from what younger women are saying, we felt God leading us to write this resource. We hope that God will use it to help well-meaning older women tweak approaches that unnecessarily sabotage their mentoring efforts.

Older women like us are sensing the change and asking how to address it. In response to this question, Barbara did her doctoral research, under Sue's supervision, on this topic, and this book is the result. As part of her mentoring research, Barbara conducted confidential interviews with young women to discover what they *really* thought about their mentoring experiences. The young women she interviewed told her about what worked, what turned them off, and why many of them desperately want mentors but end up walking away from relationships frustrated. Barbara's findings enlightened and surprised us both. The results promise to revolutionize mentoring relationships, styles, training, and outcomes. It's time to bid farewell to outdated methods and to implement new ones. We wrote this book to share what we learned, hoping to reform the way women mentor today.

In Part One, we'll explore foundational issues that explain *why* beloved but outdated mentoring methods are no longer effective. We will look at the cultural changes and fast-paced digital advancements that shape young thought and behavior but weaken the link between generations. We'll explore the new values, preferences, ideas, and problems of the next generation and how these issues impact mentoring. We'll also examine characteristics of typical older women and ways we, the older women, might unknowingly foster a disconnect that cripples what could be a life-changing experience for us both.

In Part Two, we'll get specific. You'll hear firsthand the hearts of young women pining for an older woman's nurture and guidance, but also what *they say* ruins the relationship. In response, we'll show you land mines to avoid and approaches that work today. And, at the end, we'll supply you with resources to pass on to others. Our goal is nothing less than to revolutionize the mentoring world for women, to the glory of God. It's time.

CHAPTER 1

A New Problem:
Outdated Methods

Two are better than one, because they have a good return for their labor: If either of them falls down, one can help the other up. But pity anyone who falls and has no one to help them up.

Ecclesiastes 4:9–10

Mentoring is such a need in my life. My greatest example for Christian living was my mother. But her world is not my world.

Amanda, age 32

DIFFERENT MENTORING EXPERIENCES

Through the Mentor's Eyes

Sharon scooted between cars, hurrying through the stifling parking lot to make the meeting on time. Although it was only August, she already felt the pressure of a busy fall schedule. She was unsure how becoming a mentor would fit, but involvement in the life of a younger woman interested her. At least she was willing to attend the training meeting and see what it was all about.

Refreshed by the cool air in the room, Sharon greeted friends and found a chair. Looking around at other women, she felt a wave of nervousness rush over her. *Am I even qualified to mentor?* During the next hour, she learned the requirements of the mentoring program, looked over the recommended mentoring resources, filled out a personal profile, and signed up to bring a dessert for the kickoff event. Still the question nagged: *Do I really have enough wisdom to do this?* Probably not, she thought, but her love for God and young women encouraged her to press on.

Two weeks later at the kickoff event, an eager greeter handed Sharon a bright green crayon and instructed her to find the young woman with the same color crayon as hers—"'Caribbean Green.' Isn't it peppy?" Sharon returned the beaming smile, grateful for a game to help her find her mentee. The energy-filled room lifted her spirits. This was fun! She leisurely worked the room, smiling and displaying her crayon as she went. Having found their color match, many women were already getting acquainted.

"Excuse me. I think you are my mentor." Turning toward the voice, Sharon discovered a young brunette holding another Caribbean Green crayon. After an enthusiastic hug, Sharon suggested she and Ashley visit the refreshment table and then find a place to sit down and get acquainted. Between bites of brownies and lemon bars, the women discovered they were both married to engineers, had children, were raised in the same denomination, loved to read, and had outgoing personalities. *We have so much in common,* thought Sharon. Next they visited the resource table to select a book to study together and agreed upon a time and place to meet the next week. As Sharon waved good-bye, her heart swelled with joy. She had stepped outside her comfort zone when she agreed to be a mentor, but now she was thankful. It would be rewarding to teach Ashley the things she wished she had known as a young woman.

The next week Sharon devoured the book they had picked out to study. She made notes for discussion and identified two additional Bible verses to examine. She was keenly aware of her responsibility to steer Ashley in the right direction. With her china coffee cups ready on the table, she glanced around the room one more time to verify that everything was in order for this first meeting. Ashley arrived at the appointed hour, and the women chatted for a few minutes about their week. Then Sharon prayed and they discussed the first chapter. Sharon was encouraged by Ashley's responses to the questions, observing that several important insights surfaced. They closed their time together by sharing prayer requests and scheduled a second meeting the following week. Sharon liked Ashley. She was confident they would become friends and enjoy spending time together. Over the next few days she thought about several additional topics they should study together. She enjoyed being a mentor.

Ashley canceled the next meeting. Sharon called to stay in touch but only talked to Ashley's voicemail. Four weeks later they met again, and Sharon began to wonder about Ashley's ability to keep a commitment. Sharon felt that the mentoring process would not work unless they met regularly. After meeting sporadically over the next three months, Ashley informed Sharon that her schedule was too full to continue. Perplexed and disappointed, Sharon wondered what went wrong. She knew she had done her best to offer Ashley biblical wisdom. She assured herself it wasn't personal, but feelings of failure lingered. Maybe it would go better the next mentoring term.

Through the Mentee's Eyes

"Have you thought about a mentor?" Ashley's friend inquired as she buckled her son into his car seat. "Hmm…I think I would like that. I would love to have input from an older woman who has been down this road and learn how her faith helped her handle the challenges." Ashley gave up her position as a successful corporate attorney to support her husband's lucrative job promotion, which required a move. The changes brought unexpected demands and problems to her new suburban doorstep. Should she join a firm here and continue her climb up the corporate ladder? Or should she join the ranks of stay-at-home moms? Now that both children were in elementary school, her guilt over working subsided, but she longed to explore the ramifications of these critical decisions with a woman who had been there. Ashley considered her friend's suggestion.

Ashley navigated the hallway maze looking for the sign-up coffee for prospective mentees. "Welcome!" smiled a friendly gray-haired woman. "Can I make you a name tag?" Ashley sipped coffee and balanced a pumpkin spice muffin on her knee while jotting answers on a personal profile. Another enthusiastic older woman gathered the young mentees to explain how the mentoring program would work. Then each young woman was asked to sign a covenant promising to meet regularly with her mentor over the next year, speak with and pray for her weekly, and attend a celebration tea with her when the mentoring term came to a close. Ashley hesitated. This level of commitment felt overwhelming. She already struggled to keep up with the demands of her busy life now. She doubted this was realistic. And what was a "celebration tea," and why was it necessary? She felt uncomfortable but signed the covenant because it was required to be paired with a mentor. She would meet her mentor the following week at the kickoff event.

In the intervening week Ashley had second thoughts. The process impressed her as overorganized. She was nervous about the mentor who would be selected for her. She thought about the older women she knew; some she admired, and some she didn't. For Ashley, age and Bible knowledge did not necessarily qualify a woman to be a mentor. She preferred to meet with a woman she knew, but since she was new to the area, this program seemed the only option.

When Ashley was handed the Caribbean Green crayon, she tried not to wince. Games like this reminded her of middle school. She felt awkward as she looked around the room. This might not work. She wondered if these women could understand her or the challenges she faced. Fortunately she quickly spotted the other Caribbean Green crayon, and the game mercifully ended when she introduced herself to Sharon.

At their first meeting, Ashley arrived with an incomplete lesson, but found Sharon pleasant and eager to help anyway. Sharon guided the discussion and supplied the information Ashley missed. Ashley left without mentioning the inner turmoil brought on by her recent move; it didn't seem to fit the discussion. She was now unsure Sharon was the right person to help her. During the discussion on the book, Ashley did manage to pick up the fact that Sharon lived in the same town her whole life. Could Sharon relate to her struggles with relocation? Would Sharon understand her career dilemma?

Ashley's busy schedule kept her from meeting with Sharon the next three weeks. With the insistent demands of her two children, development of a part-time legal practice, and volunteer work at the women's shelter, there was little time. With a pang of guilt, she put off meeting for another week so she could complete the lesson in the book. Sharon called, but Ashley never found time to return phone calls. The next several meetings were similar to the first. If Ashley had a question, Sharon would point to a Bible verse and tell her the right way to respond. Sharon did not seem to struggle like she did. Ashley was disappointed that after several meetings she still didn't know much about Sharon or her journey of faith.

After three months Ashley lost interest. The book was good, but she could find much of the same information on the Internet or podcasts. She liked

Sharon, but with all she had going on, meeting with her was not worth the time required. She told Sharon she appreciated her help but schedule demands would prevent additional meetings. Ashley realized they would feel awkward if they met at church. Both were embarrassed the relationship did not work out. Ashley would not try this again. She wondered if she could just find an older woman who would meet her at Starbucks and help her process life.

CULTURE MAKES A DIFFERENCE

A Sobering Statistic

Unfortunately, today many mentoring partnerships experience similar outcomes. Barbara's recent research revealed that up to 80 percent of young women abandon traditional mentoring programs in the first six months of participation.[1] What has changed? In the past, traditional mentoring methods served young women well. Multiple women mentored us, and those relationships had profound impacts on our spiritual and ministry lives. Also, we can point to other women in our generation whose lives were changed through traditional mentoring relationships. We hear their stories over and over at celebration teas. So why do fewer young women sign up for these programs now? Why don't they come forward to be mentored?

"I don't know what's wrong with young women today," remarked Donna, a longtime mentor. "They just aren't interested in being mentored anymore." Indeed, the lack of interest in traditional mentoring programs might lead one to conclude that young women have lost interest in being mentored. On the contrary, most young people today *hunger* for mentoring. Leadership consultant Michael Hyatt remarks, "If there's one thing I have learned, it's that young men and women are *desperate* for mentors who will build into their lives." Never has a generation been more open to mentoring and never has the need for mentors been greater than it is now. One twenty-five-year-old recently confessed, "I desperately want mentors. I stalk older women to mentor me. My friends and I are all dry sponges in

---

1   Barbara Ann Neumann, "An Examination of Mentoring Programs for Serving the Needs of the Postmodern Christian Woman" (D.Min. diss., Dallas Theological Seminary, 2011), 86.

need of encouragement, help, love, and listening ears." While the younger generation wistfully longs for mentors, perplexed older women pray the next recruiting campaign will bring them in.

A Disconnect

> *"My church has a mentoring program, but I wouldn't touch it with a ten-foot pole."*
>
> Alisa, age 34

The Christian community has long valued mentoring as a means to pass the faith from one generation to the next. Christian women in particular seek to carry out the mandate of Titus 2:2–3 and mentor in order to teach and train younger women in their midst. Faithful women take this responsibility seriously and labor diligently to make it happen. If young women search for mentors and older woman stand ready, what is the disconnect?

The disconnect is largely cultural. Those born after about 1965, including most of the women who seek mentors, grew up in a culture remarkably different from their parents' culture. During this time major advancements in technology changed the ways people experienced virtually every aspect of life. As a result they see, understand, and engage the world differently than previous generations. They are the product of a culture dominated by computers, the Internet, global connections, high-speed communication, continual entertainment, instant answers, constant contact, and endless information. Ideas and methods preferred by their parents and grandparents appear cumbersome and even strange to this group. Most women in this generation find traditional mentoring methods out of touch with the way they think and live. What worked for their mothers simply doesn't work for them. They want mentors but have completely different expectations for how that relationship will look.

What's Different?

> *Programs don't work for us.*
>
> Tiffany, age 28

"The society that molds you when you are young stays with you the rest of your life."[2] Even though people are individuals within that generation, they pick up common ways of thinking and living that stay with them. Value systems set in childhood are tough to dislodge. For example, many who lived through the Great Depression, the oldest generation now living, hesitate to throw away anything that could possibly be used later, "just in case." Growing up in a time of scarcity, often without basic necessities, this generation considers it irresponsible to toss out a plastic butter tub that could store leftovers. My (Barbara) eighty-nine-year-old mother recently moved to an assisted living home. When my sister and I cleaned out her clothes closet, we found dozens of belts, some dating back to the 1960s. We giggled as we tried them on, waltzing down memory lane. "They're still good!" protested my mother when we packed them up to give away. Conditioned by her childhood, she wanted to hang on to them because she might need them some day.

The younger generation has also been shaped by the characteristics of their age. When members of the younger generation toss something, their great concern is that it be recycled. They look for organic or biodegradable products that will not harm the environment. Care of the earth is a high priority, and they will most likely carry this concern throughout life. Get used to those recycle bins and going "green."

Each generation believes its way of thinking and being is the right way to live. When various generations attempt to work together, inevitable clashes over values and the best way to accomplish a task will surface. If unresolved, parties usually go their separate ways. When young women snub traditional mentoring methods, they send a clear message that they have different ideas about mentoring relationships. We can shake our heads, judge the other to be wrong, and walk away, or we can seek to understand the different points of view and design an experience that works for both generations. Understanding differences does not mean one must abandon her values or endorse a questionable ideal; it does mean she must undertake an honest attempt to respect, build bridges with, and be open to the other. If we

---

2 Jean Twenge, *Generation Me: Why Young Americans Are More Confident, Assertive, Entitled—and More Miserable Than Ever Before* (New York: Free Press, 2006), 2.

understand, we can move away from a right/wrong mentality and create mutually satisfying relationships despite our differences.

WHAT DOES THE BIBLE SAY?

People of different backgrounds and ages have always experienced challenges in their personal and work relationships. Generational conflict lurks in the shadows behind Paul's advice to young Timothy: "Don't let anyone look down on you because you are young, but set an example for the believers in speech, in conduct, in love, in faith and in purity." The situation described in 1 Timothy 4:12 indicates older people in the church discounted Timothy's instruction and leadership because he was young. Paul calls Timothy to rise above the fray and provide a godly example for everyone in the church.

A prescription for godly relationships between older and younger follows: "Do not rebuke an older man harshly, but exhort him as if he were your father. Treat . . . older women as mothers . . . . " (1 Tim. 5:1–2). Not only were the older saints to respect their young leader, but Timothy was also to honor the older ones in his speech and conduct. It is God's desire that both generations love and respect the other as He does.

You might be thinking, *That's great, but can I love them from afar?* Paul does not give us that option. Ephesians 4:1–3 further reveals God's heart. "As a prisoner of the Lord, then, I urge you to live a life worthy of the calling you have received. Be completely humble and gentle; be patient, bearing with one another in love. Make every effort to keep the unity of the Spirit through the bond of peace." When we live in this manner, we take steps toward each other, not away. We seek unity instead of separateness. Paul is saying that humility enables us to lay aside our own preferences in order to facilitate peace. God desires that dividing walls come down and women of diverse backgrounds link arms and walk together. Both generations have much to contribute to the other, and when we walk through life together, both of us experience a fuller life.

WHERE DO WE START?

But bearing with one another in love and facilitating peace can be challenging. Where do we begin? How can we bridge the gap that undermines our generational relationships? Understanding the values and preferences of each generation is a good place to start. The following are some of the generational tendencies we unpack in this book:

- Older women value programs, structure, and organization. Younger women value organic, flexible approaches.
- Older women believe you must be a positive role model. Younger women believe you must be yourself.
- Older women prefer to teach or impart wisdom. Younger women want to process life and learn from real experiences.
- Older women prefer to learn through instruction. Younger women prefer to learn through stories, experiences, and lived-out truth.
- Older women respect and trust those in authority. Younger women respect and trust only those who have proven worthy.
- Older women value privacy. Younger women value transparency.
- Older women see distinct standards for how one should live as a woman. Younger women believe there is no one right way to be a woman.
- Older women choose the mentor for the mentee. Younger women prefer to choose their own mentor.
- Older women see one mentor for each mentee. Younger women prefer to learn from multiple mentors.
- Older women prefer scheduled terms that start and stop. Younger women want an ongoing relationship and are content to build it over time.
- Older women use technology in limited ways. Younger women depend on technology to manage life.
- Older women embrace contractual commitments. Younger women continue only if the experience is valuable.

A quick scan of this list verifies what many of us already know—the generations often have a substantially different outlook on life. You'll find these different perspectives reflected in next generation responses at the end of each chapter.

This admittedly oversimplified description of the two generations attempts to capture broad trends. When assessing people it is tempting to stereotype individuals unfairly and miss unique individual characteristics. The authors recognize there are exceptions in both groups and this list will not accurately describe everyone; however, Barbara's research shows these are typical preferences that impact the practice of mentoring and explain the decline in mentoring relationships.

AN URGENT NEED

When the busyness of life and stress of ministry catches up with me, I (Barbara) often retreat to my backyard garden. I take particular pride in my tiny strawberry patch. Unfortunately, a nocturnal creature appreciates it as well and steals the ripe berries just before I can harvest them. To foil my four-footed adversary, I placed netting over the strawberries. One morning I went out to harvest berries and found a frog caught tight in the netting. There was no struggle left in his limp body, and I could tell he had given up. He didn't appear to be the likely strawberry thief, so I cut him loose and he gratefully wobbled off.

Just like that frog, many mentors are caught up in an outdated model. They struggle to make it work and eventually give up because they don't know what needs to change or how to change it. For over three decades, we've mentored women and led ministries with women. During recent years, we've observed that demand for mentors is higher than ever but traditional endeavors sit idle due to lack of young participants. And when young women like Ashley do participate, far too many leave unfulfilled and disappointed. We grieve when mentoring relationships fail unnecessarily. Parties limp away wounded and the church suffers.

It is incumbent on mature women of God to break through the impasse and bring young women back to vital mentoring relationships. We must find ways to retain one of the most valuable tools for spiritual growth. Join us on a journey to discover how to create vital mentoring relationships that work today. The first step is to understand and appreciate younger women. Read on.

I keep trying to be involved in traditional Bible studies and mentoring relationships, both in my church and in other Christian organizations. I really do try! But my attempts keep coming up dry, for so many of the reasons mentioned in this chapter. Either I get creeped out by the idea of being forced to "share" with a mentor I don't know, or I find the material for a "Bible study" wearisomely, repetitively about "proper women's roles," or I join a Bible study to find it stiff and isolating. Sometimes I actually join and stick it out, but most often I just shy away from joining something that has all the trappings of being a disaster, or I end up dropping out because my incredibly busy schedule simply cannot absorb an event that is not truly feeding me.

In the end, though, I don't feel good about not being involved or about dropping out. I keep wanting to tell someone, though I'm not sure who, that I'm not trying to be difficult. Would anyone believe that? I'm not sure they would. I feel difficult. And it's lonely.

Mariah, age 36

Before now, for several years when I was going through mom's death and trials in court, I sought out women to talk with but found none. I was usually sent to the pastor of the church when all I really wanted was someone to listen and care about me. There was one lady from my hometown I would get to talk to every once in a while, but when we did get to meet, it was so refreshing to my soul. I cherish it to this day. However, it is difficult when you live in different states. I just remember craving that kind of relationship, but God is sufficient and took care of me Himself.

Stephanie, age 31

CHAPTER 2

A New Generation: Understanding Postmodern Women

Our society is in the throes of a cultural shift of immense proportions.
Stanley J. Grenz[1]

Things are no longer merely in the process of change; things, my friends, have changed. And by things, we mean everything."
Craig Detweiler and Barry Taylor[2]

For my generation older mentor-type women may be kind of outdated because this is a new generation, a new world, and we do things our way."
Hollie, age 27

"**I really don't know about** this next generation," a frustrated older woman confided. Anxious for a sympathetic ear, Carolyn recounted her recent experience as cohostess of a baby shower with several millennial women. A veteran shower hostess, Carolyn suggested the women meet to plan the event and coordinate responsibilities. "Why do we need to meet?"

---

1   Stanley J. Grenz, *A Primer on Postmodernism* (Grand Rapids: Eerdmans, 1996), 173.
2   Craig Detweiler and Barry Taylor, *A Matrix of Meanings: Finding God in Pop Culture* (Grand Rapids: Baker, 2003), 24.

inquired one of the young women. "We'll just text you and tell you what we will bring." Other heads nodded; coordinating their busy schedules for a meeting would be difficult. Carolyn was caught off guard by this minimalist approach. It was important to match the color of the invitations, napkins, plates, flowers, and name tags, as well as assign duties and ensure the proper serving pieces would be available. This approach was unsettling. All well-done showers start with a planning meeting.

Realizing she was outnumbered, Carolyn said, "Okay, I guess I will get the cake." Another young woman chimed in, "We don't need a cake. Everyone is on a diet and it won't be eaten." Another setback. A shower is not a shower without a pink or blue cake decorated with the appropriately colored baby booties. To her dismay, Carolyn began to realize this shower would not follow the traditional format. The young women went on to arrange details through texting and email while Carolyn worried about loose ends.

An hour before the shower, the young hostesses arrived at Carolyn's home to set up. At best, it was organized chaos. As they chatted and worked around each other to arrange the food table, a forgotten ingredient sent one hostess scurrying off to the store. Carolyn was sure she would not return in time and the table would be incomplete. Another hostess discovered her serving dish was too small for her fruit salad and wondered if she could borrow one from Carolyn. Carolyn left her task to search for a suitable serving bowl. Still another hostess needed a serving utensil. Carolyn left her task again to locate her large engraved silver spoon. When the first guest crossed the threshold, the now tense Carolyn looked with amazement on an attractive table with everything in place.

"It all came together," Carolyn admitted, "but I don't think I can do that again. It was just too nerve-racking." Stressful situations like cohosting a shower play out many times when older and younger women attempt to work together or embark on a mentoring relationship. Carolyn experienced firsthand just how different the values and preferences of the generations can be. But is giving up on joint ventures the answer? Should we stay with our own kind to keep everyone's blood pressure down?

Imagine if one of these young women asked Carolyn to mentor her! What obstacles might plague their relationship? How could they prepare for a meaningful mentoring friendship that could enrich both their lives? Unless both women learn more about generational differences, a mentoring friendship is unlikely to thrive.

THE POSTMODERN GENERATION

Those who track societal trends agree we are experiencing a tsunami of cultural shifts:

> Every few hundred years in Western history, there occurs a sharp transformation. . . . Within a few short decades, society rearranges itself—its worldview, its basic values, its social and political structure, its arts, its key institutions. Fifty years later, there is a new world. And the people born then cannot even imagine the world in which their grandparents lived and into which their own parents were born. We are living through such a transformation.[3]

The world has moved right under our feet. Most of us were unaware of this profound societal shift, but many women *did* notice that relating to their teen or young adult daughters became more challenging. Somehow the rules changed and both became aware of a deepening divide. "Mom, you just don't get it!" was heard in more than one household to the consternation of both parties, now sharply alienated. Dedicated moms and grandmothers are genuinely mystified by the obvious disconnect. This problem shows up outside families as well. Sixty percent of employers report misunderstandings and tensions between the generations in the workplace.[4]

Next generation women do not intend to be difficult—they were simply born into a prominently postmodern culture. Broadly speaking, *postmodern* indicates the time that followed the modern era. The modern age began in the 1500s and lasted until about 1980. By the 1980s the Internet, personal

---

3   Peter F. Drucker, *Post-Capitalist Society* (New York: Harper Collins, 1993), 1.
4   Jean Twenge, *Generation Me: Why Today's Young Americans Are More Confident, Assertive, Entitled—and More Miserable Than Ever Before* (New York: Free Press, 2006), 217. Twenge's book is the result of twelve studies on generational differences and is based on data collected from 1.3 million young Americans.

computers, and advanced digital technology became available to the general public, instigating rapid changes and new worldviews that prompted Western society to "rearrange itself." People born during this time grew up in a new context, were molded by a new culture, and have a markedly different set of beliefs about themselves and the world they inhabit. You may be thinking that Postmoderns will eventually grow up to become like their parents and grandparents, but most of their beliefs and tendencies are not likely to change as they age. Postmoderns live in an environment vastly different from the one their mothers and grandmothers knew, and this difference prompts the disconnect we now see.

Since most of the women who seek mentors are part of the postmodern generation, the practice of mentoring is significantly affected. These young women often wonder why older women do not understand their interests, deep needs, and problems. In this chapter we explore postmodern trends and identify some of the new values, preferences, ideas, and challenges of the younger generation in order to better understand and develop these precious women.

Gen Xers and Millennials

Before considering the values and challenges of young women today, first we need to understand that the postmodern generation is composed of two distinct groups. Think of the generations as pigs moving through a python. Those born around the same time (the "pig") move through the python together and experience seasons of struggle and influence based on local, national, and world events, fads they have enjoyed, and prominent people they identify with. The first "postmodern pig" was followed ten years later by a second "postmodern pig." Although they are close to each other, there was sufficient societal change during that short time to create some differences, or two somewhat different pigs; however, both pigs have postmodern characteristics overall.

The older members of the postmodern generation were born sometime between 1965 and 1981. They are commonly referred to as Gen X, but may also be referred to as Busters because they busted the birthrate set by their Boomer parents. This generation is much smaller than the generation before and after it.

When I (Sue) teach generations in my seminary courses, I call Gen Xers *the wounded generation* because they are the first generation of latchkey kids. During their childhood the divorce rate tripled, and mothers joined the workforce in massive numbers. Many saw their parents make huge sacrifices as they attempted to climb corporate ladders or achieve the American dream. Typically, these children felt neglected and now display cynical attitudes, the result of a series of broken promises. They are willing to work hard but refuse to sell their souls to the company the way their parents did. They prize freedom and many are commitment-leery when it comes to marriage and family. They crave healthy relationships and long for the home they never experienced, but winning their trust isn't easy; however, if you do earn their trust, your influence will be huge.

The youngest members of the postmodern generation were born between 1982 and the early 2000s. They are usually referred to as Millennials because they are the first adult generation of the new millennium. Other labels include Gen Y, Always On Generation, iPhone Generation, Generation Next, Generation We, Emerging Adults, and Bridgers because they form a bridge between two centuries. But when abcnews.com asked Millennials to label themselves, they suggested "Don't Label Us"—a peek into this generation's propensity to customize everything.[5]

Many Millennials spent their early years in minivans with signs announcing "baby on board," with mothers who doted on them and fathers who attended their births and coached their Little League teams. These kids were told, "You are special," and "You can do anything." Their helicopter, or constantly hovering parents insisted kids receive trophies just for showing up. And now that their children have entered the workforce, some of these parents hound HR and demand that their Johnnie or Susie get the raise they think they deserve. As a result many Millennials carry a sense of entitlement.

These kids are optimistic, tech-savvy, and confident. They work well on teams and are civic-minded and inclusive, and we'll probably see all kinds of glass ceilings break as they take charge in the future. But we have a concern that many aren't prepared for the real world, and when they learn they

---

5   Neil Howe and William Strauss, *Millennials Rising: The Next Great Generation* (New York: Vintage, 2000), 6.

can't run the company after their third year on the job, they will need wise mentors to help them adjust.

Both these groups of young women value spirituality, but many have a skewed view of Christianity, which they characterize as fake, legalistic, intolerant, unloving, too politically enmeshed, and boring. Also, many see the church as a patriarchal institution, where women are not honored or given opportunity. For a potential mentor, these are serious roadblocks to overcome. Worth the investment, many of these young women hunger to understand who God is, how He works in the world, and what it means to be loved by Him unconditionally. They need you desperately, and if you earn their trust, your influence can change the course of their lives. What a privilege!

These two generations share many of the same values and challenges that we discuss at length later in this chapter. But you may also notice some differences between these two groups of young women.

Disclaimer

As you consider who these women are and why, remember that every young woman is God's unique creation and some will exhibit these characteristics more than others. Young Christian women steeped in religious traditions often display both modern and postmodern characteristics. Personality, gift-mix, background, and ethnic and cultural influences also affect a woman's identity, belief system, and worldview. We both raised two daughters in Christian homes. Although profoundly impacted by our modern values, all four young women exhibit some of the qualities and perspectives described below.

Our desire and fervent prayer is that the following concepts will help you mentor, appreciate, love, respect, and bear with the Postmoderns that God asks you to shepherd.

POSTMODERN VALUES

Relationships

This generation is relational to the core. They long for genuine personal and social connections. They yearn to be part of an authentic community where they belong and experience acceptance. Home life for many Postmoderns felt like a whirl of activity. Parents busy with their own careers and activities found little time to support equally busy children and teens. Home was the place you caught your ride to the next enrichment activity. Young women's desire, and sometimes obsession, for warmth, stability, and belonging drives many of their choices because of the high value most place on friendships; however, the vital connections they seek are more difficult to make today. Lifestyles that fostered community disappeared along with the typewriter and wall phones. Today, connecting through the Internet, social media sites, and texting may keep a woman's personal life in front of her friends, but in reality the typical Postmodern tends to have few personal relationships and remains strangely isolated. For all its benefits, technology has made daily life impersonal. We'll say more about "techno-isolation" in Chapter 8.

Longing for genuine community and relationships is one of the strengths of the postmodern generation. They remind us that God created us to live in community and be part of one another's lives. Instead of sliding into the back row to remain anonymous, these women want to immerse themselves in a real community that will nourish their souls and help them flourish.

Education

Millennials are America's most educated generation. In 2011 almost 70 percent of high school graduates enrolled in college. When broken down by gender, statistics reveal that 72.3 percent of female graduates enrolled in college as compared to 64.6 percent of male graduates.[6] Women now earn 58 percent of undergraduate college degrees and half of the degrees in law and medicine.[7] Also, studies show that women students are more motivated, get better grades, are more likely to complete their degree, and earn more honor degrees than men. These statistics do not reveal a decline for men; they continue to perform about the same. What has changed is women's performance.

More education opens doors of opportunity to young women, allowing them to make significant contributions. Today many are likely to be as confi-

---

6   Bureau of Labor Statistics, U.S. Department of Labor *News Release*, April 19, 2012 (http://www.bls.gov/news.release/pdf/hsgec.pdf).
7   Twenge, *Generation Me*, 189.

dent and assertive as their male colleagues. Now the majority of accountants, financial managers, medical scientists, and pharmacists are female.[8] Also, competent young men and women work comfortably alongside each other to accomplish tasks in their professions as well as in their personal lives. For many in the younger generation, equal opportunities in education and industry have dissolved a number of traditional gender roles. Today, for couples between twenty-five and thirty-nine, only 28 percent of husbands are the sole provider.[9] Growing up in a culture where equality between the sexes is a given, young women expect a significant and active role in whatever they undertake. In the postmodern world, jobs, including those in marriages, are typically assigned to the most qualified person instead of according to gender. Their educational background and preference for lifelong learning means these bright women are a great resource for the Christian community, and it's important to hear their voices and utilize their talents.

If you are a mentor, don't expect all younger women to view gender, work, and marriage roles the way you do. If you encounter differences, you will need to consider how to respectfully navigate these challenges for the good of the overall relationship. Furthermore, if you are considering mentoring, limited educational opportunities and experience may cause you to wonder if you can relate to, or even help, a younger woman with more education than you have. Reject these thoughts. Postmoderns are not looking for a mentor to "teach" them as much as a mentor who will share life with them. One young research participant expressed it this way, "I wish more of the insecurities of older women would just be killed already! I hate seeing so many older women think they have nothing to give, and that they don't know what to do with a girl like me."

Tolerance

Constant exposure to global events, foreign cultures, and all types of religious faiths leads Postmoderns to value diversity. Since childhood they were told that all discrimination is wrong. Raised in the self-esteem movement and taught everyone is unique and special and must pursue his or her

---

8   Ibid.
9   Ibid.

own dreams, these young adults readily accept different ideas and lifestyles. They respect other cultures, traditions, and worldviews, and many prefer a multicultural group of friends. Perhaps this is also because the younger generation is the most diverse in American history. Immigration altered the Western landscape, placing people of various nationalities in their neighborhoods, classrooms, and workplaces.

Recently, while dining at a trendy restaurant, I (Barbara) noticed a cheerful, and noisy, group of young women seated near us. Celebrating a girls' night out, they hugged, chatted, and laughed nonstop. What struck me was the diversity of the crowd; it looked like the United Nations. Five different ethnicities gathered around the table. Postmoderns' global awareness erases prejudices held by previous generations and allows them to embrace people outside their own ethnicity, tradition, and community. Because they are comfortable with and accept outsiders, Postmoderns make strong additions to outreach teams. Many mentors can profit from an intimate friendship with a younger woman who has learned to love and enjoy all people, regardless of external differences.

Experiential Opportunities

Growing up in highly visual and interactive learning environments created new learning preferences for young adults. As tots they learned their numbers as they counted along with the gently spooky Count on Sesame Street. In kindergarten they worked on interactive computer screens. Lifelike images dominated their video games in middle school. In high school they searched the Internet to complete school assignments in groups. For them learning is interactive, collaborative, visual, and experiential. Many prefer to learn through hands-on experiences, images, and art rather than through traditional, information-based instruction.

Because this generation is experiential, they also tend to learn more through stories than lectures. They will listen to lectures, but are moved by stories that speak to their experiences and engage the heart. In a frequently chaotic world, stories help them make sense of their experiences. They want to tell their stories and hear others' stories, especially ones that show how God has been at work. In mentoring relationships, telling stories is a great way to build bridges across the generational divide. When a mentor listens intently to a young woman's story, the young woman feels validated, supported, and encouraged. When she hears an older woman's story, she considers new possibilities that generate hope. If you are a mentor, you probably learned to value formal teaching methods in your school years, and you may think that telling stories is a waste of time. Don't you believe it! Postmoderns love and learn from your stories.

Working with young women can be rewarding because many are creative, outside-the-box thinkers and bring fresh perspectives to the table. When stuck recently on a ministry problem, I (Barbara) called on a millennial woman to help me out, and her familiarity with technology gave me several new options to consider. Older, seasoned women certainly know a great deal, but they can also learn new, effective ways from these innovative young women.

Flexibility

Because typical young women lead demanding, busy lives, they expect flexibility from others to make their crowded schedules work. Most labor hard to keep up with work, participation in church, community service, marriages, and children. More and more young women opt for jobs that offer flex hours or stay-at-home options so they can keep all the balls in the air. Rigorous schedules leave little time for meetings with mentors, despite Postmoderns' hunger for mentoring relationships.

Because they value flexibility, often young women will respond unfavorably to the mentor's suggestion that they meet at the same time each week, or even weekly. Many older women like to plan their calendars ahead. We feel that a regularly scheduled time shows commitment to the relationship and fosters intimacy. But this highly scheduled approach makes many young women feel misunderstood and managed. From their perspective, the older women seem clueless or insensitive to the many demands on their time. We discuss ways to work through these differences in Chapter 5.

Making a Difference

Many in the younger generation are not content to simply live in their community—they want to *invest* in their community locally and worldwide. This passion manifests itself in various ways: helping renew parks and neighborhoods, volunteering on behalf of victims of injustice, eliminating sex trafficking, providing educational opportunities for the disadvantaged, care for orphans and refugees, and providing clean water in developing countries. They believe that they are called to be part of a solution for these problems. Although usually somewhat commitment adverse, these young ones are quick to commit to a cause that allows them to impact the world in positive ways. They volunteer at a higher rate than any other generation.[10] Since they also started the recycle and green living movements, products aimed at the eighteen to thirty-nine demographic often tout their earth friendly features. Postmoderns share a deep concern for the health of the planet and its resources and expect responsible behavior from all its inhabitants.

Typically, Postmoderns aren't as committed to the local church as their parents and grandparents, and many prefer to participate in kingdom work outside the church. Dedicated postmodern leaders start food pantries, coffeehouses, pregnancy support ministries, tutoring centers, and businesses to assist people in their own communities. Instead of overseas destinations, these young women are more likely to see their own neighborhoods as the mission field.

Organic Options

Postmoderns support the organic movement, now a 14 billion dollar a year industry.[11] This popular movement values natural over contrived, simplicity over complexity. In addition to organic products, this generation values an organic way of life, one that happens more naturally, informally, and with less structure. For these women, life is not neat and tidy, and not everything must match or fall carefully into place. They expect life to be messy and tend to avoid situations that feel too contrived, overorganized, or rule heavy. Instead, these women are more attracted to simple and natural opportunities to learn and grow. The younger woman's preference for organic options will influence how a mentoring relationship looks and functions.

---

10 Howe and Strauss, *Millennials Rising*, 215.
11 Georgia Clark, C. Parr Rosson, Flynn J. Adcock, Dwi Susanto, "The New Horizon for Organics: A Market Outlook for the Effects of Wal-Mart on the International Organic Market," Center for North American Studies Department of Agricultural Economics, Texas A&M University, June, 2007. http://cnas.tamu.edu/The%20 New%20Horizon%20for%20Organics.pdf

Authenticity

Not only are the best products natural, the best people are natural. When asked about the ideal relationship with a mentor, young Heather responded, "In the postmodern world, we want honesty over rightness. Get to the heart of things—be open, honest, raw about your life. None of this formality stuff; let's just get to the heart of the matter." Heather demands authenticity. She and others like her have built-in authenticity detectors and can quickly sniff out a phony. Their byword is *keep it real*.

Mentors, listen up! Younger women learn from mentors who are honest about their failures, hurts, and struggles. They are suspicious of women who seem too perfect and believe it is more important to be yourself than to make a good impression. This movement toward authenticity has encouraged many women, regardless of age, to admit their needs and share their journey of spiritual transformation with others. If you are a mentor, younger women yearn to help you through your life struggles, just as you assist them through theirs.

Development of Self

The manner in which Millennials spend the decade of their twenties is one of the most remarkable departures from their parents' generation. For their parents, completion of college meant a career and family, but when Millennials exit college, they are eager to experience the endless possibilities before them. Told they could be anything they want to be, they often dedicate their twenties to the discovery of just what that means. They see this decade as a time for exploration, adventure, and development of personal identity. Traveling to other cultures to live and work is often part of this grand experiment.

Wherever they work, they expect a meaningful life outside of work, and they will often turn down opportunities that require excessive time on the job. But we wonder how global economic volatility will impact their expectations and hinder their dreams. Mentors may need to help them adjust to a world that is not quite as full of possibilities and adventure as they were led to believe.

Living in the postmodern world may mean young women no longer accept a uniform standard for what it means to be a woman. Young women now feel qualified to pursue any dream as they see traditional roles fade into the past. The process of self-discovery means adulthood, traditionally considered the time for commitment and settling down, is postponed until age thirty or even later. There are four times as many single women in their early thirties as there were in 1970; and four times as many women give birth to their first child after age thirty than in 1975.[12] These statistics indicate that the primary life goal for more and more young women is no longer traditional marriage and family. Mentors need to be cautious about assuming every mentee dreams of white picket fences and baby carriages.

Collaborative

Equal opportunity environments trained young minds for active participation. Postmoderns have never known anything but an open-source world, or an environment where everyone is allowed to give input. Almost everything posted on the Internet today solicits user input. Sales sites practically beg customers to give them a rating. Blogs routinely conclude with an invitation to add your thoughts to the discussion. Hotels and other service venues anxiously monitor feedback sites where a negative evaluation can make or break them. Wikipedia, the mega information source, is a collaborative endeavor built on user contribution.

Life in an open-source world means Postmoderns expect collaborative environments that allow them to make contributions. Young women hunger for meaningful opportunities to use their gifts and participate in God's work. These expectations dramatically alter the dynamics for vibrant mentoring.

Value Added

A young woman is a woman on the go, and time is her most precious commodity. She lives in a cacophony of events that clamor for her attention, and in order to maintain some sense of equilibrium, she must sort out which ones deserve her attention. She cannot assign value to everything, and in the end, her limited time will be allocated to events or opportunities that contribute the most value to her life. Whereas her mother or grandmother felt a sense of duty to support traditional Christian activities, she is motivated less by duty and more by outcome. Her life is all about "value added," and

---

12 Twenge, *Generation Me*, 189.

situations that fail to measure up will fall to the axe. An older woman must consider that her mentee's "time economy" may be vastly different from hers and adjust expectations accordingly.

Spirituality

Unfortunately, since Postmoderns grew up in a time of widespread corruption in the church, many are lukewarm about organized religion. But the good news is that they remain interested in issues of faith and spirituality. They may not attend church regularly, but young women still search to discover a meaningful life with God. Many long to know who God is, how to connect with Him on a simple, natural level, and how to experience His presence in everyday life. Eager to go deep and discover transformational power, they see faith as something to be experienced rather than confessed.

Comfortable with the mysterious nature of God and faith, they are particularly skeptical of platitudes, pat answers, or standardized formulas designed to methodically develop spiritual maturity or solve problems. For them faith is an often-messy process, and freedom to express doubts and wrestle with spiritual issues in an environment of acceptance is vital.

Mentors raised to view church loyalty and attendance as a requirement of all real Christians may chafe at the younger generation's lack of commitment, but don't allow this difference to sink the relationship. As a mentee grows in faith, she will hopefully learn to value the church as Christ's body on earth.

CHALLENGES FACING POSTMODERN WOMEN

If you are a mentor, we hope you are now convinced that young women are capable, vibrant, creative, accomplished, and *different* from you and other women in previous generations. However, the differences involve more than values and preferences; young women also face new challenges.

Skeptical of Authority

When interviewed for our research, all the young women indicated they were reluctant to be paired with a mentor they did not know. What is behind this previously unseen reluctance? Respect for a mentor is not automatic—it must be earned. This rule applies to teachers, employers, public figures, and people in the church. In their opinion, it is more than age or availability that qualifies a woman to mentor. They look for a mentor who has lived an authentic life or possesses traits they admire. What draws one young woman may not attract another. This reserved attitude toward older women makes pairing of mentor and mentee a challenge and impacts how mentoring relationships form. We discuss options in Chapter 4.

Overscheduled

Raised to be busy people, most postmodern women keep their schedules full—really full. I (Barbara) was recently checking out at a small grocery store when a harried young woman brought her items to the front. Seeing I would take another couple of minutes, she asked the attendant to open another register so she could check out and still retrieve her cat at the vet and make pickup time at her child's school. She had no time for pauses. The extra few minutes in line behind me would have derailed her afternoon. Keeping schedules chocked full can lead to a pace that is eventually unsustainable. As a result, Postmoderns may habitually run on empty and battle depletion, stress, and depression.

Single women usually don't fare much better. They must work to pay their own bills, and work often follows them home or demands exhaustive travel that hinders an enjoyable personal and social life. Married friends and family sometimes assume that, since they are single, they have more time than others to volunteer, help out friends, or care for family. Single mothers are burdened by overwhelming responsibilities and need mentors too.

We teach and minister to female seminary students. Many are Postmoderns who pack their schedules to the brim with work, family, ministry, and a demanding course load. Burnout is common, yet many of these students yearn for mentors too. Most mentors will be asked to help younger women figure out healthy life loads and rhythms, but ironically we may be forced to do so in a more rushed format or shorter sessions than we might prefer. But don't assume that quick haphazard meetings are necessarily unproductive in a younger woman's life.

Anxious

Everything is relative. At least that is what younger women were taught. They heard, "Choose what works for *you*, what *you* believe to be true." Her belief might be different from the person next to her, but no problem; everyone's values are legitimate and acceptable. This philosophy breeds many "truths," all of which put forth different standards for a meaningful life. All of the "truths" bouncing around mean that in the end one must simply choose the truth she likes the best. No wonder young people are often confused. Their culture sends mixed messages that create dissonance in the human mind, and they must navigate life in a sea of relativity that keeps them off balance. InterVarsity leader Jimmy Long explains that life for those in the next generation is like trying to stand on a fast moving train with nothing to hold on to.[13] As a result, many Postmoderns are left searching for direction in life but hold a faulty compass. Which road will lead to joy and stability? Without certain truth, the only way to find out is to try the roads one by one and deal with the disappointing dead ends they often encounter.

Add to this the fact that many well-meaning parents burdened their children with impossible expectations. The culture tells them they can do great things, their parents expect them to follow through, but the real world often throws up roadblocks to greatness. The blockbuster television show and singing competition *American Idol* interviewed one of the female contestants who managed to secure a coveted place as a top-twelve finalist. "It's really true," the seventeen-year-old contestant bubbled. "You really can be anything you want to be if you believe in yourself and want it badly enough." Never mind that *thousands* of contestants were turned away from the show even though they believed in themselves and wanted it badly. The ubiquitous promise rang hollow for them as they watched their dreams crash. Many others likewise find that roadblocks or limitations of one sort or another prevent them from achieving their optimistic goals. Unprepared for the harsh realities of life once they are on their own, Postmoderns now commonly experience a midlife crisis between the ages of twenty-five and thirty. [14]

Young women experience an additional stress—the ticking of the biological clock. Those ticks get louder in their thirties. They may have previously postponed marriage or pregnancy, but for many women, marriage

---

13   Jimmy Long, *Emerging Hope: A Strategy for Reaching Postmodern Generations*, 2nd ed. (Downers Grove, IL: InterVarsity Press, 2004), 165.

14   Alexandra Robbins and Abby Wilmer, *Quarterlife Crisis: The Unique Challenges of Life in Your Twenties* (New York: Penguin Putman Inc.), 2001.

and family are now high on their priority list. But again, circumstances may be unfavorable for achieving these goals as they anxiously watch their childbearing years slip away.

For these and other reasons, Postmoderns identify anxiety as the number one problem in life.[15] What a great opportunity for older women to come alongside and support, encourage, and guide young women when they encounter confusion, roadblocks, and dead ends.

Morally Lax

With relativity in full swing, those who teach moral values are labeled politically incorrect, naive, and intolerant. Who is to say what is right or wrong, and on what basis? Therefore, the voice of the culture says it is better to remain silent on moral issues and let each individual make her own decisions. After all, relativity insists that what is right for me may not be right for you. As a result, many young people were required to figure out their own moral values, and many did so without the guidance of parents or teachers. This mind-set plays out most noticeably in areas of sexuality where just about anything goes—sex at frighteningly young ages, one-night stands or "hooking up" with casual acquaintances, abortion, homosexuality, and cohabitation. Unfortunately for many young women, experimentation with premarital sex left them with a string of bad experiences and wounded hearts. Mentors must help women deal with the scars of promiscuity and guide them toward a new biblical moral framework, as they help young women understand why these standards are in their best interest.

Wounded

The breakdown of the family means many in the postmodern generation are children of divorce. It is difficult to overestimate the effects of divorce on these young lives. Shuttled between parents and houses, these women have little concept of an intact family and the community and security it normally provides. For them, normal means a blended family with stepparents and stepsiblings. One young woman commented, "It really gets interesting when your grandparents divorce and you get stepgrandparents." Hurting hearts

---

15 Twenge, *Generation Me*, 104–136.

need the healing balm of God's forgiveness and grace, and loving mentors have a unique opportunity to apply this balm and facilitate healing.

Coarse Language, Tattoos, and Piercings

When Sylvia and I (Sue) met for coffee, she told me her story, peppered with expletives and "potty" language. She described her abusive stepdad who labeled her a tramp when she was still a child, as well as his constant sexual innuendoes. In high school, she ran with a rough crowd, became sexually active, and had a demon tattooed on her back. But Jesus rescued her, and now her eyes danced as she expressed her love for him.

Admittedly, her crass language jarred and irritated me. I wanted to shout Colossians 3:8 in her face: "But now you must also rid yourselves of all such things as these: anger, rage, malice, slander, and filthy language from your lips." But I was certain that our definition of filthy language was different and scolding would only have distanced her. Over time, as she walked with the Lord, she used vulgar speech less and less, but it still erupts occasionally when her emotions take over, when she wants to make a dramatic point, or when her peers join us. Her view of civil, modest, and clean behavior doesn't match mine.

I sensed God leading me to offer her my unconditional love and later teach her proper standards. Grace needed to come first. Mike Shepherd, a pastor to Postmoderns in Denver, says it well:

> We use the term *grace* a lot in church lingo. That word taught us that everyone matters to God and should matter to us no matter what his or her struggle is in life. One thing Postmoderns do is freely admit their struggles. It can be pretty raw and shocking at times as they share their struggles, from homosexuality to maxing out credit cards. Sometimes four letter words are used. But that's okay. Remember, you are there to mentor them. Our goal is to take them from where they are in life when they come to us to where God wants them to be. It takes patience, genuine care, and real acceptance to walk with them on that journey. It can take years. But that real acceptance will lead to trusting relationships that can then lead them to trust Christ and become followers.

We must extend love and grace to all regardless of where they may be in life and provide a safe place during life's challenges.[16]

Now Sylvia keeps the demon tattoo covered, and her new tattoo is 2 Corinthians 5:17: "Therefore, if anyone is in Christ, the new creation has come: The old has gone, the new is here!" Now that's real progress.

By the way, 39 percent of Millennials sport a tattoo.[17] Why are tattoos so popular with Postmoderns? Tattoos are an outward expression of their inner selves, a way to show off their different sides. They use them to communicate their uniqueness and tell the story of how they view themselves. "It is so important to be an individual, and to communicate that fact to others, that young people routinely tattoo it onto their skin."[18]

SUMMARY

In a nutshell, Postmoderns tend to be attracted to relationships that fall naturally into place and are unlikely to be part of anything that places programs or structure ahead of organic relationships. With their educational background and information only a click away, they find information-based programs uninspiring. They will also ignore methods that appear to turn out cookie-cutter women. Busy lives require a fluid mentoring process rather than one based on a contract. Their preference for authenticity means older women can no longer talk primarily about principles or hypothetical situations. They must be willing to honestly share their own faith experiences.

Younger women see mentoring as a collaborative partnership instead of a relationship where wisdom flows from one to the other, and they expect to participate in the development of the mentoring relationship. Most importantly, they will stick with the mentoring relationship *only* if it adds value to their life.

---

16 Mike Shepherd, "Keepin' It Real," *Gifted For Leadership* (2013): 21.
17 Allison Pond, Gregory Smith, and Scott Clement, "Religion Among the Millennials," Pew Research Center, February, 2010. http://www.pewforum.org/2010/02/17/religion-among-the-millennials/
18 Twenge, *Generation Me*, 97.

Now that you understand a little more about young women, you probably grasp why traditional methods have lost their appeal. But there are more generational realities to discover. Before we can build relational bridges we must also understand our own tendencies and why it may be hard for us to make adjustments. In the next chapter we discuss the preferences of modern women and why Postmoderns often struggle to understand us.

I've wondered about participating in a mentoring program, but it gives me anxiety to think that it might not work out. I'd hate to hurt someone's feelings or get stuck in a mentoring relationship that isn't helpful. I agree that most Millennials are very hungry for a mentor. It's difficult because we are very busy, and it must be worth our time. That sounds selfish but it is true!

Sharon age 32

I met Linda at a church, but she was older than me, so I didn't really know if we'd have anything in common. I have tattoos and don't mind showing 'em off. Then I saw her on Facebook and thought I'd see if she wanted to grab lunch with me sometime and hang out. I wasn't sure how it would go. She agreed and we talked about everything from family issues to past relationships and work. I liked how real she was. I told Linda about a recent incident where pictures of me in lingerie ended up on Facebook. I had them done by a female photographer, just as a confidence-boosting thing for me, and then they ended up on the Web. I was freaked! But then I started getting some positive comments, and it actually ended up helping my body-image issues. About halfway through telling Linda my story it dawned on me that she could really judge me for having those pictures done in the first place, but I could tell she was just taking it all in and really listening, so I kept going. She didn't say a whole lot, just encouraged me that body image is a struggle for so many women and that I wasn't alone in it. She talked about her own struggles and mentioned that Jesus had really helped her in that area. It was something I thought about a lot after we met.

Jolie, age 23

CHAPTER 3

A New Challenge: Understanding Ourselves

*Willingness to embrace change is a key difference between great or-
ganizations (including churches) and those that are willing to settle
for mediocrity and eventually become obsolete. You may think you're
doing people a favor by keeping things the same to keep people happy,
but many times what's comfortable isn't what's healthy. Organizations
need to change. Relationships need to change. People need to change.
We hate change, but we need to change.*

Tony Morgan[1]

*Similarly, the young—whether in physical or spiritual years—are
many times not a primary focus in our planning. While their youth-
ful energy is admired, other facets of their lives are foreign to older
women. The impulse is to influence them to live in the comfort zone
of the previous generation . . .*

Beverly Hislop[2]

---

1   Tony Morgan, comment on "We Hate Change. We Need to Change." Tony Morgan
    Alive blog, comment posted June 24, 2011, http://tonymorganlive.com/2011/06/24/
    we-hate-change-we-need-to-change/.
2   Beverly White Hislop, *Shepherding a Woman's Heart: A New Model for Effective Minis-
    try to Women* (Moody: Chicago, 2003), 121.

*Women in the older generation are a complete mystery to me. Women
in my generation look at them and say, "Why are you like that?"*
Ginger, age 28

As Lesa exited the church building, the dialog of a con-
tentious meeting still swirled in her head. The time had come to shut down
the mentoring program. Although demand for mentoring was still high,
she was weary of the struggle to make it work. As a pastor's wife she had
led the mentoring ministry for over a decade, but her current relationships
with young women convinced her that any mentoring initiative going forward required a new approach.

It wasn't always a struggle. In the beginning she simply matched a
young woman with an older woman she knew well. But the church grew
and she no longer had a feel for the character and experiences of many
of the older women. Next a mentoring team tried to match women
based on profiles. They prayed for God to help them connect women
based on some commonality, but way too many train wrecks resulted.
Lesa wasn't sure how to proceed, but she did know this—it would look
different. Two needs dominated her thoughts: the need for mentoring
and the need for change.

UP FOR THE CHALLENGE

The US military is one of the most highly adaptive organizations in the
world. Keen minds continually assess global situations and the best way
to meet hostile challenges to North America in the twenty-first century.
The military is aware that today their fighting force is composed mostly of
postmodern men and women, and they design tactics and strategies with
this young generation in mind.

One example is the recent war in Afghanistan. The enemy's weapon
of choice is the IED (Improvised Explosive Device). US convoys roamed
Afghan roads looking for expertly hidden IEDs to disarm before they could
do their deadly damage. These bombs were too dangerous for a human to
approach directly, but a young soldier could sit some feet away in the safety
of an armored vehicle and send out a small robot. In the soldier's hands,

he held a Nintendo Game Boy remote control, the exact same one used in popular video games. With this remote, he expertly maneuvered the robot to disarm the bomb. Instead of requiring soldiers to learn a new technological control system, the military understands it's more effective to leverage technology that their young soldiers know well. Training time is minimal, the soldier is confident, and the mission is accomplished.

In a similar adaptive move, in March 2012 the US Marine Corps developed a new ad campaign designed to appeal to Millennials' desire to improve life for people globally. Long known as "the first to fight" and "leathernecks who like to break things," the Marines' new campaign now promotes their humanitarian side. YouTube videos, TV spots, Facebook, and movie trailers show Marines distributing food, water, and medical supplies to suffering people in devastated villages. The message: Marines are people who work to right injustice, fight tyranny, and alleviate suffering. While this campaign is unlikely to impress retired Marines drawn to serve by a sense of patriotism, duty, and self-sacrifice, it does capture the attention of young men and women who wish to travel the globe and make a difference in the world.

Resilient organizations get outside themselves, observe from different angles and perspectives, and make necessary changes to remain viable. Perhaps these adaptive organizations that depend on postmodern participation and talent for national security are on to something: to mentor young women we must consider who they are, we must understand who we are, and we must be willing to change.

WHAT DOES THE BIBLE SAY?

A Time to Understand

King Saul's body lay slain on Mount Gilboa, abruptly ending his forty-year reign in Israel. The shocked nation gathered quickly to install new leadership. Most leaders believed God's choice was thirty-year-old David, the man the prophet Samuel had anointed years earlier. Energized men from all over the nation met in the town of Hebron to support David and transition to a new government. Most of them arrived heavily armed, ready to fight anyone who opposed David with a rival candidate; however, a small contingent of men arrived with wisdom instead of weapons. These were men from the tribe of Issachar, "men who understood the times and knew what Israel should do" (1 Chron. 12:32).

They brought an understanding of the times, an ability to correctly discern the meaning of the current situation in Israel. In the midst of a nation changing by the moment, they helped David recognize what adjustments needed to be made for Israel to move forward under his leadership. David apparently listened to their advice, valuing their insight as he united twelve formerly independent tribes to forge a strong nation for God.

Mentors Who Understand

Like the US military and the tribe of Issachar, effective mentors today must understand *our* times and discern the implications for mentoring. Able to see the different angles and gripped by a new vision, they notice what others miss. They look beyond their own familiar borders and see new possibilities that include women of all generations. They understand the impact of generational differences, but they also see how to build connecting bridges and initiate new approaches to mentoring that work today.

They correctly discern where a yielding spirit is needed, without ever abandoning the truths of the Bible or timeless approaches that are still effective. Like the men of Issachar long ago, women who want to shepherd and grow young women today must learn to appreciate the changes required to wisely move forward.

Young women hunger for a new generation of mentors who understand the times and care enough to consider what works for them. One young woman expressed the need this way: "I was going through a bad time with my husband and needed someone to talk to. I tried to reach out to the mature Christian woman who led my small group, but I think I scared her. She was not ready for my honesty, although she did try."

From Scary to Aha!

Claire Rains helps us understand the typical disconnect between the two women in the previous example. She writes, "Establishing rapport is based on the principle that *people connect with people who are like them.* [3] Based on this principle, it is clear why the older woman mentioned above found the interaction with the younger woman scary. Because the two women were unlike, the interaction was awkward and a connection unlikely. In all probability the older woman operated out of a set of social norms that caused her to be uncomfortable with such a frank approach. She found herself in strange territory, unsure how to respond, and both women left the encounter uneasy. Sadly, this older woman was not ready for a wide-open opportunity to mentor. Now is the time to get ready and we want to help you. Young women desperately need mentors to help them find the way forward—they need you. But first you must understand yourself as well as the young women God calls you to shepherd.

In the previous chapter, we discussed typical ways young women understand the world. It is vital that mentors understand the different perspective of young women, but that is only half the picture. It is equally important for mentors to know how *they* were shaped and the unique ways they understand and respond to the world around them. Mentoring should not be scary. When mentors understand who they are and why they think differently, fears dissipate. We hope that the following characteristics of older women will generate a few *Aha!* moments for you.

A Caveat

Before we look at typical characteristics of the modern generation, we need to address resistance you may be feeling right now. When I (Sue) teach my seminary courses using research studies that seem to pigeonhole people, I know I will encounter resistance from some students. I feel that apprehension too. Each of us is a unique individual regardless of the generational name we bear. And we are complex creatures. Personality traits, heritage, spiritual gifts, learning styles, leadership styles, experiences—all these and many other factors play into who we are. No research study can label any of us accurately.

Then what is the value of research studies and assessments that seem to place us in one category or another? They provide generalizations that

---

3   Claire Raines, *Connecting Generations: The Sourcebook for a New Workplace* (Rochester, NY: Axzo, 2003) 34.

help us understand broad realities. They show us people's tendencies, and that awareness is helpful as we attempt to discern how to live well in this complicated world.

As we describe different characteristics of modern women in the rest of this chapter, some qualities will probably describe you and others won't. My mother was born in 1918, but she was different in much of her thinking and behavior from the majority of women who were born around the same time. For example, she adopted the feminist attitudes of the generation that followed her, yet she refused to throw away rubber bands and butter tubs, like so many of her generation who lived through the Great Depression.

We must not interact with others based strictly on cookie-cutter analysis. Nevertheless, studies that discover tendencies are extremely valuable as we attempt to discern how to understand, help, and love one another. These characteristics tip us off to likely qualities and explain why different generations tend to think and act differently in light of key events, family and relational health, economic factors, political systems, and social and religious shifts. But no one fits these categories completely, and some people may not fit any of them. Still they can be enormously helpful when understood as bents, predispositions, or inclinations. Just don't pigeonhole yourself or the younger women you mentor. Keep that caveat in mind as you consider what research has discovered about the typical traits of modern women.

THE MODERN GENERATION

Just as the younger generation is often referred to as *postmodern,* people born before 1965 are commonly referred to as *modern*. Many women who mentor fit this category. We use the term *modern* to describe the era before the postmodern era, or the time period before the digital age. Many people use the term *modern* incorrectly today. For example, my (Sue) ninety-year-old mother chose Mod Moll as her email handle, thinking that this handle made her look cool and with the times. In reality, she dated herself. Modern is no longer correctly used to describe something new. The modern era is past, and we are now living in the postmodern era.

Women who reached adulthood before the digital age think differently than Postmoderns do. They respond to a different set of internal instincts. While the younger generation's perspective on life is significantly shaped by technology, the thoughts and convictions of the modern generation were shaped largely by the sixteenth-century Renaissance and the Enlightenment age. This period in history is also known as the Age of Reason and dominated Western culture and thought for five hundred years. These two movements, the Renaissance and the Enlightenment, ushered in a "modern" era that elevated the principles of science and the power of human reason over mystical and spiritual forces that were formally thought to control the world and people's lives.

Fueled by the excitement of discovery, Moderns undertook scientific investigations that gave birth to archaeology, the examination of the fossil record, advancements in medicine, the delivery of water to parched lands, space exploration, and many other quests that dramatically improved life for countless people across the globe. We owe much to the modern mind.

Molded by the scientific method, typical Moderns tend to be logical, orderly, efficient, and linear thinkers. For many of us, the world operates according to scientifically proven principles, and we believe this approach yields reliable formulas that improve our personal lives and solve complex problems.

Modern Values

Individualism

While the postmodern generation tends to place high value on relationships and community, many of us Moderns possess a powerful individualistic streak. Raised in a culture that taught us that dependence on others reveals weakness, we Moderns tend to be self-sufficient. Thus, some of us find asking for help difficult, maybe even humiliating.

Some Moderns attend a church service and leave without speaking to anyone. Since many of us attend church to gain biblical knowledge and meet individual needs, fellowship with others can be optional. We tend to be loyal members, regular attendees who support the church, but we tend to lack meaningful relationships with other congregants. We often need to be coaxed into community. As a whole, we Moderns are less inclined than Postmoderns to see the value of community to enrich life.

Because we tend to be individualistic, many of us expect mentoring to be a one-on-one relationship. Individualist thinking also convinces some of us that we must be adequate to meet all the needs of a mentee. Unfortunately, this expectation to be an all-wise resource leads some of us to believe that we are not qualified to mentor.

Individualism can be a problem, but it also has inherent strengths. Often, we Moderns can focus, work hard, and put in extra hours to get the job done because it is more than a job. It reflects on our personal competence. This motivates us to do our best.

Structure, Rules, and Organization

Typical Moderns prefer well-ordered environments where nothing is left to chance. We were steeped in the reliability of proven formulas and believe careful procedures guarantee a good result. Life for many of us Moderns works better when diligently organized and managed. As one modern ministry leader commented, "I always have a backup plan for my backup plan."

Rules enable situations to run smoothly and efficiently, while structure and schedule keep programs strong and enable us to achieve our goals. Top-down meetings are necessary to disseminate information, assign duties, and make sure everyone is on the same page. When typical Moderns work on a project, we look for immediate results and tend to have little patience for situations or relationships painfully slow to develop. For many of us, the best way to meet needs or accomplish goals is to organize an efficient, well-run program.

Organization and structure definitely have their place. Thanks to the organizational talents of Moderns, diverse ministries touch people and meet needs around the globe. It is not hard to see why most modern women prefer to mentor through a well-organized program. Pairing mentor and mentee seems to be the efficient way to provide every mentee with a mentor. No one falls through the cracks. Specified and regular meeting times assure that everyone stays on the same schedule. Rules ensure a quality experience. If you want a job done on time, with discipline and accountability, recruit a Modern.

But this approach fails to attract most postmodern women. It collides squarely with their preference for informality, flexibility, and organic options. Young women resist what feels like *too much* structure. They have reasons why they feel this way that make sense to them. We'll explore these reasons in later chapters.

Knowledge and Information

Many of us are inclined to believe in the transformational power of knowledge and formal instruction. Because many of us prefer to learn this way, we often consider teaching a specific book or curriculum the best path to spiritual growth. Thus, to many of us, mentoring is largely formal Bible teaching.

The modern woman's love for the Bible is remarkable. We treasure God's Word and value Bible study as a way to know and serve God. Our love for serious study has fueled many scholastic endeavors and contributed a remarkable body of scholarship to the Christian community. Our generation has placed Bibles in many hands, and as a result many people in our generation are familiar with the Bible's content and message.

However, when it comes to mentoring, young women will often tell you they can get Bible study or teaching in a number of places, so they look for a different experience in mentoring. One morning I (Barbara) walked into a church office and greeted a young woman working at a desk. Facing away from me, she did not answer. I bent around to catch her attention and saw her iPod plugged into her ear. She pulled out the earpiece and explained that she was listening to her favorite Bible study teacher and didn't hear me. This is now the norm. Quality biblical instruction is only an iPod away, but mentoring is harder to come by.

In my research on mentoring, I (Barbara) asked young women how they learned best. Many replied that stories, personal experiences, and lived-out truth were more powerful "teachers" than formal study and instruction. They learn godly habits by watching how another woman lives. Curriculum-based mentoring programs that center on Bible study or biblical topics, as good as they may be, often fail to interest young women; however, these young women *are* eager to learn how to live a godly life, and they *are* interested in how the Bible informs that life.

It is important to clarify that both of us (Sue and Barbara) teach at a seminary and believe Bible study is of the utmost importance. God's Word is foundational to all we know and do as believers. Sue authored a curriculum of in-depth Bible studies entitled *The Discover Together Series*. We wish everyone would study the Bible more, for its treasured revelation can never be adequately plumbed. The question we want to pose is this: is formal instruction the only way to teach biblical truth to women who want to see how faith works in ordinary life? They ask us to share our lives first and then show them what an incredible difference God's Word has made. Older mentors need to recognize that the mentoring approach that worked for them may not be the best approach for the next generation.

The Best Role Model

Postmoderns insist on authenticity in relationships. This presents a special challenge for those of us who were taught to be good role models, the kind of woman others could look up to. Sadly, many of us were taught that we needed to be perfect. Makeup, hair, nails, clothing, children, meals, laundry, coffee, house, dog (you get the idea)—all expected to meet some high standard. We can remember when a run in your pantyhose meant a wardrobe disaster and a frantic run to the store. That run ruined our appearance. And, oh yes, pantyhose were required so our legs looked perfect.

Many of us give the impression that we have it all together (shoes, purse, hemline, and earrings perfectly matched and not a hair out of place) because imperfection is failure and failure is unacceptable. From a modern perspective, it's best to play it safe and keep up personal appearances. That means personal failures are kept private. That way others continue to see us in a good light. Convinced we should be good role models, we usually limit personal sharing to admirable behavior.

Although some Moderns show encouraging progress on this front—more of us sharing our personal stories—our first tendency is still to keep mistakes private. This tendency creates serious problems in a mentoring relationship today. Why? Because Postmoderns don't *trust* women who pretend they don't make mistakes or have problems. To young women, a refusal to be real appears plastic, unapproachable, and uninteresting. If you do not overcome your tendency to wear a mask, you will kill the mentoring relationship. If only we understood how much our honesty could encourage a young woman and make her faith journey come to life!

Commitment

Just say the word "commitment" in a room of Moderns and Postmoderns, and you'll feel the tension. Commitment may be the most conflict-producing issue between modern and postmodern women. We believe people should be able to count on us and responsibility is part of good character. A person of integrity makes and keeps commitments. We accomplish important things when we make and keep commitments. It only makes sense that mentoring is more effective when mentor and mentee commit to one another. Relationships are built through commitment. Or so many of us older woman are convinced.

One mentoring leader was overheard saying, "It's important these young women learn to make a commitment. That is why we have them sign a mentoring contract. They should see it as a privilege to keep this commitment." Many young women's reluctance to make commitments is an ongoing source of irritation for older woman.

Our conviction rises from a sense of loyalty and duty, wonderful character traits. But will the younger woman see it this way? Think about her busy life and the "value added" rule. She does make and keep commitments, but they are based on value added, not duty or contracts. For her, connection through mutual attraction leads to commitment. These connections have the potential to develop into deep, lifelong friendships, but they cannot be forged through a contract. A new way to think about mentoring.

Spirituality

A quick Sunday morning scan of a typical North American church service reveals that Moderns occupy the majority of seats. While many Postmoderns are lukewarm about the organized church, Moderns are churchgoers and the backbone of the church. We believe Christianity includes church membership and regular attendance. Typically, we admire and trust church leaders and believe our obligation is to give money, serve God, and serve others through the church. In fact, we Moderns keep the traditional church alive today.

For many of us Moderns the focus of the church service is the sermon. We come to hear biblical teaching and to learn. We often apply the scientific ideals of correct procedure and proven formulas to spirituality. We consider the Bible the divine textbook for correct faith and practice, and we thrive on sermons that offer practical spiritual principles for successful Christian living. Many of us gather during the week to study the Bible, or to study books about biblical subjects. We like to discuss what we learn in small groups but are usually more eager to hear a lecture that increases our understanding of the Bible or the right way to live. Studies by polished, professional speakers are especially popular because we tend to believe Christian growth is fueled by knowledge.

We are also drawn to conferences, seminars, and retreats led by well-known Christian leaders. As part of her research Barbara interviewed a church staffer who led a mentoring program. She paid a significant amount of money to bring in a big name speaker for a young women's mentoring event. She was seriously annoyed because the young women were not motivated to attend and the event was a bust. "I can't believe they wouldn't come!" she sputtered. "That is just unbelievable!" Maybe not if you understand that postmodern women, unlike their modern sisters, are unimpressed by big names. They would rather learn how to be spiritual from the ordinary but faithful women around them.

Our approach to spirituality is another disconnect for typical young women. From the young woman's perspective, many of us rely too heavily on facts and instruction as transformational elements. Our faith seems more like a correct belief system than a personal journey with God. Instead of looking for fact-based teaching or steps to spiritual success, the young woman is hungry to experience the living God. She sees the Bible not as a textbook with different parts to be analyzed and studied in order to live correctly, but as the way to know and connect with God. She is interested in the whole story of God and how she fits into that story. She can't relate to principles, formulas, or pat answers for complex human problems. She prefers to wrestle with tough issues in the context of faith, and she is particularly resistant to approaches guaranteed to work if practiced correctly.

Although we each favor a different emphasis, the spiritual preferences of both of us have potential to come together in marvelous synergy. The young woman can benefit from our love of Scripture and passion for communicating its power. We can benefit from her desire to experience God. Both of us have genuine spiritual strengths needed to serve God holistically.

In Summary

When we modern women mentor, our values and preferences come into play. It makes sense to us that mentoring should be through an organized program that is structured, scheduled, requires commitment, has a teaching focus, and emphasizes Bible study. This works in our world, and we naturally think it will work for younger women as well. In fact, this mentoring method did work well for many years. But now the task is to build on the accomplishments of the faithful and godly mentors who went before us as we adapt their methods to the needs of today.

MODERN WOMEN'S CHALLENGES

Many of us bring helpful knowledge, reliability, and experience to mentoring. But just like the younger generation, we modern women face unique challenges.

Inflexible
Some of us can be heard saying, "But we've always done it *this* way." Many of us tend to believe if a method worked well in the past, why change it? Reliable methods are, after all, reliable. Clinging to past methods becomes even more attractive when a preferred method is elevated to "God's method," and those who propose change are thought to work against God.

Yes, some things should never change. For example, the truth of God's Word, the sufficiency of the gospel of Jesus Christ, and the command to make disciples never change. But methods to accomplish God's work can change and should change. The *message* never changes, but *methods* continually change so faith can be passed effectively from generation to generation.

If we stubbornly resist change, young people consider us frustrating to work with. Many Postmoderns consider some of us locked in to routine methods that blind us to needed innovations. Some even suggest that a clean sweep of Moderns from leadership is the only way to make progress. How unfortunate, because we bring a ton of experience to enrich most every situation . . . if we aren't inflexible.

Sandwiched
Many of us find ourselves sandwiched between the Greatest Generation (our parents), and the postmodern generation (our children). Quality healthcare and healthy lifestyles have extended life expectancy and enabled people to live well into their eighties and nineties. But when elderly parents can't

manage life on their own, many Moderns must step in to care for them. At the same time, more and more postmodern children are returning home after college, depending on their parents for support. These situations create financial and emotional stress for those of us who find ourselves sandwiched. Unfortunately, sandwiched women feel they are unavailable to mentor due to extra family responsibilities that deplete them.

Unavailable

When life slows down some of us want to take a deep breath, relax, and focus on ourselves. An empty nest is not all bad—suddenly there is "me" time. For many years some of us put family and other responsibilities above our own needs and interests. So when the chicks fly, we want to jump up and down, wave a flag, and shout, "Now it's my turn!" Many of us return to school to earn the degree that had to wait. We reenter the workforce full or part time. We pursue opportunities that allow us to develop our spiritual gifts. While Postmoderns "find themselves" in their twenties, we often do this in our fifties or sixties. For some of us, part of this self-discovery means we are through meeting the needs of others, we have "been there and done that," and we leave the ranks of ministry volunteers. Or we are simply too busy to add another responsibility to our schedule.

Younger women pick up on the attitude that some of us lack the inclination to invest in them. One young woman put it this way: "I wish there was more of a desire among women my mom's and grandmother's age to mentor girls. Sometimes I feel like older women just don't want to. My generation is ready and waiting but there aren't any mentors."

Christian artist and blogger Randy Elrod expressed this same frustration when he asked the probing question, "Where Are the Female Mentors?"[4] This lament was prompted by his young-adult daughter's desire for a mentor at a crucial time in her life. He suggested several women he knew well. "I listened in disbelief as she related that each one told her *no*."

---

4   Randy Elrod, comment on "In Search of Heroes—Where Are the Female Mentors?,"
     Randy Elrod, comment posted February 5, 2012, http://www.randyelrod.com/in-
     search-of-heroes——where-are-the-female-mentors/.

Elrod, a men's mentor for over eleven years, observed that male mentors are also in short supply, but "there is a disconcerting and disproportionate dearth of female mentors." Sadly, many of our older godly women are content to leave the important work of passing on the faith to someone else.

Insecure and Perfectionistic

Many of us grew up in a culture where some considered females inferior to males. Appreciation for God-given gender differences was pretty much nonexistent. Navigating through a male dominated society produced feelings of inadequacy in some women. Some of us also grew up in homes where parents were quick to point out our shortcomings. Many of us are still confused about what it means to bear the image of God as a woman, and we struggle to feel complete in Christ.

Postmodern women tend to be more confident and are mystified by the insecurity they see in their older sisters. They are largely unaware of the battles against marginalization modern women courageously fought to create the atmosphere of equality and acceptance that postmodern women enjoy today.

Feelings of insecurity can easily give birth to perfectionism, or an obsessive need to be flawless. An overly critical attitude toward herself and others identifies a perfectionist. She attempts to live up to unattainable standards and expects others to do the same. Perfectionists live in a control tower that manifests itself in meticulous attention to detail, impossible standards, and creation of a high-control atmosphere in order to ensure a perfect result. Perfectionism often leads to unrealistic expectations and burnout. The reality is that we are all finite humans in process. Until we accept that truth about ourselves and others, and let go of perfectionistic ways, we won't thrive in life or in a mentoring relationship.

Don't confuse perfectionism with excellence—striving for excellence is admirable. Pursuit of excellence is different from perfectionism in that it pursues high standards, but leaves room for mistakes and even expects them. We speak as recovering perfectionists and know the struggle, but we have experienced the marvelous benefits of releasing control.

Perfectionism is a turnoff for many Postmoderns. They prefer to learn from women who know how to relinquish control to God, as expressed in this young woman's words: "The women of your generation who have let go of control are the ones who make me want to follow Christ more. The faith of a woman who is trying to control everything is not attractive. It puts a postmodern woman at ease when they give control to the Lord." Instead of being impressed, many young women see modern women's attempt for perfection as over-the-top endeavors that create a stiff environment. "All my mentors are not perfect women and they don't claim to be. That's why I picked them." Perfectionism in a mentoring relationship leads young women to suspect that their mentor will be judgmental of their imperfections. Loving others well and perfectionism are seldom compatible bedfellows.

Divorced

If you were born between 1946 and 1964, according to generational experts, you are a Baby Boomer. Your generation experienced a higher divorce rate than any other, and recent research shows the divorce rate in this generation is still climbing.[5] While Boomers normalized divorce, those separations still generated significant pain. Many of you traveled a dark valley of grief, rejection, self-doubt, lost hope, emotional instability, shame, failure, and financial insecurity. If you divorced and then remarried, you often faced the challenge of blended family.

Time and strength are required to overcome the effects of divorce. If you have been divorced, you may still carry the wounds years later and feel that you have little to offer as a mentor. You fail to understand that many younger women also endure the sting of broken relationships and families. When I (Sue) ministered at a women's seminar in Oregon, my teaching was followed by a panel of postmodern seminary students. I'll never forget the raw words of one young woman, "I've never experienced a home. I've never sat down with a family to a meal together. I need to know how to get through my loneliness and lack." A woman who's been there, one who has learned to cope and even find joy, can be a tremendous help to women who share the same feelings.

---

5   National Center for Family and Marriage Research, FP-12-05, "Age Variation in the Divorce Rate," http://ncfmr.bgsu.edu/pdf/family_profiles/file108695.pdf.

MORE ALIKE THAN DIFFERENT

By now we hope you grasp some of the sources of misunderstanding and irritation between modern and postmodern women, often resulting in a disconnect. Yes, we face challenges, but women of all generations have more in common than it might seem:

- Love for God and salvation through Jesus Christ
- Desire to be godly women
- Need for relational connection
- Ability to relate to the image of God in another woman
- Unique ability to understand the language and needs of another woman
- Unique ability to relate to the experiences of another woman
- Unique ability to encourage, teach, and learn from each other

In spite of generational differences, women know best how to understand and meet each other's needs. Paul told Titus to prepare the women in the church at Crete to train and equip one another (Titus 2:3–5). Titus was qualified to minister to the women, but Paul told him to delegate this responsibility and privilege to mature women.

Throughout the ages, God trusts older women to come alongside younger women, to love and inspire them and help develop them into strong, godly women. But first, we older women must intentionally learn to understand younger women and find healthy ways to accommodate our differences. Only then can we follow God's mandate to mentor the next generation. God's reputation and the health of His church are at stake.

We've explored why outdated mentoring models no longer work, and we've examined characteristics of both Postmoderns and Moderns to help us better understand ourselves and the women God entrusts to us. But what does mentoring this new generation look like and *how* do we do it? Part Two offers practical suggestions.

My Sunday school teacher is an incredible woman who tries to be a mentor to all the women in our class. She is forty years older than me! I'm proud of my teacher for being the kind of older woman who listens to our stories without judgment, but because of the generation she comes from, I'm not sure she always knows how to respond. She never shares any personal experiences about her own past mistakes. So, sometimes I look at her and think, "Maybe she never made any," even though I know that isn't true. It makes it harder for me to share my struggles with someone who seems to have never had any. I'm much more likely to tell my struggles and flaws to a peer, who I know experiences some of the same challenges. It helps younger women to know that the women in the previous generation have gone through the same things we're going through. If we don't hear that, we have a tendency to feel bad about ourselves and wonder why we can't have the faith and strength these seemingly "perfect" women have. I love, love, love the older women in my life, but the ones I share the most of myself with are the ones who share the most of themselves with me.

Holly, age 28

Part 2

A New Approach

Introduction

It's time to bid a not-so-fond farewell to the old paradigm and move into the twenty-first century. We need to redefine what mentoring truly is and then redesign how we go about doing it.

David Stoddard[1]

A VISION FOR MENTORING

If redesign is needed, what must change? The Uncommon Individual Foundation, an organization for mentoring research, reports that after marriage and family, "mentoring is the third most powerful relationship for influencing human behavior."[2] Third most powerful, that is, if the relationship works. If you are reading this book, chances are you have a keen interest in fostering influential mentoring relationships with lasting impact. You care enough to consider a redesign.

How do mentor and mentee find one another? What determines the frequency of their contact? What should they do during the times they share that will most effectively help younger women become all God designed them to be? Does mentoring have to be one-on-one? We'll explore other formats that may work just as well. Social media is a part of a younger woman's life. What part should it play in the mentoring relationship? We will address these and other critical questions in the pages that follow. Remember that some changes in your expectations and approach could be the difference in a mentoring flub or a faith-builder that will change a young woman's life, as well as the lives of those who come behind her!

---

1   David A. Stoddard with Robert J. Tamasy, *The Heart of Mentoring: Ten Proven Principles for Developing People to Their Fullest Potential* (Colorado Springs: NavPress, 2009), 23.

2   Larry Kreider, *Authentic Spiritual Mentoring: Nurturing Younger Believers Toward Spiritual Maturity* (Ventura, CA: Regal, 2008), 12.

CHAPTER 4

A New Focus: Initiating a Match That Works

All those years of recommendations, I felt like I was conducting a blind-dating service, hoping a match made in heaven would result. What I longed for was a new approach that would take the burden off the mentor and simplify mentoring.

Julie Pierce[1]

These women entered my life because of my needs. They had attributes I craved, and they were kind enough to come alongside and teach me from their journeys. . . . I believe we seek out mentors because they have in their lives an element we want.

Carol Brazo[2]

---

1   Julie Pierce, comment on "Using the '2 Steps' Method to Simplify Mentoring," Empowered By Pierce blog, posted May 12, 2013, http://empoweredbypierce.com/using-the-2-steps-method-to-simplify-mentoring/?utm_source=Blog+Subscriber%3A+Friday+Favorites&utm_campaign=9a76ba1b37-Friday_Favorites_from_Empowered_by_Pierce4_17_2013&utm_medium=email&utm_term=0_a328a6e-b8a-9a76ba1b37-354594433.

2   Carol Brazo. *Divine Secrets of Mentoring: Spiritual Growth Through Friendship* (Downers Grove, IL: InterVarsity Press, 2004), 21.

It's not one of those things you can just sign up for. This isn't a pot-luck. It's just not. Don't try to control it. Let the mentee come to you.

Amy, age 23

Maribeth, thirty-two and single, steadied her Starbucks and settled into the black leather couch opposite me (Barbara). Although she was raised in a Christian home, in high school Maribeth drifted far from her faith. After college, the gap widened again when she took a job in another part of the country, far from the support of family and hometown. With God pushed to the margin, she made choices she now regrets. But she's back, hoping for a fresh start and eager to grow in Christ. A year ago, she determined that a mentor could help her figure out how to integrate her professional career and her Christian life as a single woman. I was there to listen to her mentoring story.

"I wanted a mentor so I signed up for the mentoring program," Maribeth explained. "They paired me with a mentor, but we were very opposite. It was strange, very uncomfortable, and right away I knew we weren't off to a good start. That was *not* a positive experience for me." Unfortunately, I hear this over and over in conversations with young women—strange, uncomfortable mentoring experiences.

On a mission to understand, I encouraged her to elaborate. Maribeth continued, "I called and told the woman leading the program, 'Hey, this isn't going very well.' And she said, 'Well, we prayed over this match a long time.' And I'm sure they did, but I knew right away it wasn't working. I am not one to quickly throw in the towel so I did give it a good effort, but sometimes people just don't click."

Maribeth sensed a mismatch with her assigned mentor almost immediately, and if we could hear from the other woman involved, she would probably agree. A critical element was missing—the compulsory click. The women who arranged the match felt divine orchestration was more important than a comfortable connection between mentor and mentee, so they advised Maribeth to carry on despite the click's absence.

Maribeth tried to make it work, but the relationship felt forced and ended up a bad experience for both women. The awkwardness of this relationship convinced Maribeth to stay away from "random" matches in the future.

"Yeah, I'm not doing that again," she confided. "More often than not I hear that the pairing up doesn't work very well." Thankfully, she refused to give up on mentoring altogether and later found a mentor on her own, a person with whom she felt more comfortable. For Maribeth, and for most young women, some kind of click between mentor and mentee is a must.

The Compulsory Click

What exactly is a click and why did its absence sink this relationship? A click is an intangible something that occurs when a mentee and mentor are drawn to one another. A natural, comfortable relationship follows, combined with excitement and anticipation. It's what happens when you warm up Mom's apple pie and top it off with scoops of best-quality vanilla-bean ice cream, or Washington's best apple slices with chunks of gourmet cheese, or spiral-sliced ham topped with a fruity glaze that brings out the best in all the ingredients.

It's like chemistry. Heat potassium chlorate to a melting point, add a red gummy bear, and stand back. When the two come together you get light, heat, and fizzling gas. (Don't try this at home.) Incredible energy—or synergy, the interaction of two forces so that their combined impact is greater than the sum of their individual parts. When chemistry is evident, you sense that God will use this relationship in both your lives for His good purposes, and the possibilities excite you.

The relationship needs to be comfortable from the beginning, a foundation on which to build. Then it turns into something rich and sweet. We've all experienced this type of natural fit with the discovery of a close friend or perhaps our mate. It's hard to say exactly how people are drawn to each other in romance or friendship. Complex elements are often unknown even to the people involved. They simply recognize a click when it happens and the relationship naturally takes off.

Choosing a young woman's mentor for her is like trying to choose someone's close friend or mate. Most of us can remember a time when we thought two people would be perfect together, maybe even arranged for them to meet, only to have it go nowhere. The two unfortunate people involved probably spent most of the time politely looking for an escape hatch. Similarly, if a click is absent, a mentoring relationship is flat and doomed. For next generation women mentoring is all about the click.

Making a Successful Match

Research indicates that this initial click significantly impacts the success of the relationship.[3] When we step back and think about it, often we are pairing strangers. In the past, well-meaning older women, hoping to help the mentoring process along, set up programs that looked something like this: women interested in forming mentoring relationships signed up. Third parties set up rules for the relationship; meet once a month, call one another once a week, meet for a year, choose a curriculum, and so on. Then the women who organized the program used their best personal knowledge, informative surveys, and prayer to pair a mentor and mentee. They notified the pair, expecting them to contact one another.

Twenty years ago, I (Sue) led similar programs in my role as minister to women in several megachurches. Some matches between women worked, but more didn't. When they didn't, we were left with tears, wounded hearts, and bruised psyches. The hours spent "mopping up" were not worth the good that resulted from successful relationships. In time, we discontinued the programs, but the pleas for mentoring continued, leaving us bewildered.

When Barbara interviewed young women who had participated in these kinds of programs, they described this pairing approach as "scary." As one young woman explained, "It is a scary thing because you don't know her. You aren't sure if the person who matched you really knows if you'll fit well. You depend on her opinion that you would be great together, but it's based more on where she thought God was leading than what you know about yourself or the other woman. It's scary to walk into that." Not exactly the start we want.

Even though the matching approach is well thought out and well intentioned, it's still scary to the young women we hope to reach. Why? She's afraid of a no-click situation with no way out—we seldom offer escape hatches as part of these programs. As one young mentee insisted, "I want to know something about this person. I want to know where she came from. I want to know who she is." Considering what we now know about

---

3   Ray Pawson, "Mentoring Relationships: An Explanatory Review," ESRC UK Center for Evidence Based Policy and Practice (Working Paper 21, 2004): 2.

Postmoderns from Chapter 2, it should not surprise us that her idea of a strong start looks different than ours. Instead of a blind match, she prefers to start with a woman she already knows.

As Moderns, we may think this preference gums up a perfectly good process. This new "click" wrinkle slows down the process. As one doubtful mentor countered, "But if we don't pair them, mentoring doesn't happen." She has a point. If mentor and mentee are not paired, how does this relationship ever get off the ground? It's time for fresh thinking and a more organic approach.

We admit that many of us may find the changes we recommend uncomfortable. They are not systematic, organized, predictable, or measurable. But mentoring isn't about our preferences. It's about building into the lives of a new generation of women who need Jesus desperately but won't find Him unless we forgo outdated mentoring methods. Though organic mentoring feels looser and unorganized, we still have this going for us: young women desperately seek mentors. They want this to happen even more than we do. We simply need to discover a way to start that makes them feel safe.

Trust Comes First

The starting point for most next-generation women is trust. The trustworthy character of a potential mentor is more important to Postmoderns than whatever the two women might have in common. Even if we tell her that a particular woman is trustworthy, the typical postmodern woman won't accept our endorsement. She is only convinced by firsthand observation. Dallas pastor Matt Chandler put it this way: "If you have people signing up to be mentored and then you pair them, the miss rate is really high. You cannot just throw people together who don't know each other and expect to see a deep bond form."[4]

Both Sue and Barbara love to mentor, but we know not every woman will connect with us. Recently I (Barbara) was asked by a friend to mentor a struggling young woman. We didn't know each other, but it was one of those

---

4   Matt Chandler. "The Good Fight: On Sanctification, Making War Against Sin, and Cannibalism in the New Reformed Movement." *Leadership Journal* (September 8, 2009), under "How is this different from a mentoring program?" http://www. ctlibrary.com/print.html?id=84712

situations where my friend just knew it would work. She introduced us and the three of us chatted over coffee. It seemed to go well, and the potential mentee agreed to meet with me again. Two weeks later my second cup of coffee grew cold as I waited for her to show up. I never heard from her again. I can't say this was entirely unexpected; I thought it might go this direction since she did not know me well enough to trust me with her struggles. Although I am a seasoned mentor, we were "thrown together" and it didn't work.

For postmodern women mentoring starts with trust, so a potential mentor must be a person she already knows. She may not know her personally, but the potential mentor has in some way demonstrated a worthy life, a skill, or credibility the young woman admires. Since a click is nonnegotiable for young women, a relationship of knowing, even if it is just observing from a distance, is necessary *before* a match.

Attraction Is a Must

Trust makes a mentoring click possible, but it's only the first step in a successful start. Since motivation is also critical, trust must be accompanied by natural attraction. After studying the matching process, researcher Ray Pawson observed, "Good old fatal attraction is hardly something that can be predicted and encoded into programme (sic) planning."[5] We can try hard to be observant, and sometimes we do correctly predict attraction, but too often we miss the mark. When attraction is present, women enjoy spending time together and experience a more satisfying and productive mentoring relationship.

What do we mean by "attraction"? We know it when we experience it. For example, when I (Barbara) recently upgraded my cell phone, the salesman convinced me to purchase a cover, one that would protect my phone in almost any catastrophe. "This is the one you need," he said, pointing to the package. Although it was ugly, I knew this practical option was the safe choice. He indicated this cover would even allow my phone to float in water, although I was unable to think of a single scenario where that might actually occur. So I walked away with my phone encased in a bulky vinyl overcoat.

---

5   Pawson, "Mentoring Relationships," 2.

Some time later while shopping with my daughter, I experienced immediate *attraction* to a jeweled pink peacock phone cover. I picked it up and admired it closely. We bonded. But the over-the-top bling warned me it was too heavy to float, so I reluctantly returned it to the shelf. Regret followed me home.

A month later my daughter's Mother's Day gift arrived, and yes, the box contained the resplendent peacock cover. Good old fatal attraction motivated me to recklessly discard the practical plain cover and snap on the glamorous new one. The power of natural attraction prompted a choice based on a feeling deep inside. I didn't really want safe; I wanted glam. If my phone ends up in a toilet, I will deal with it.

Now, not everyone has the same attraction to blingy peacocks that I do, and most people wouldn't predict this as my choice. I probably look more like the practical, phone-floating type to someone else. Or maybe someone else would find phone floating important to *her* and assume I would agree. But for me, it was peacock all the way, even though I tried to make the other "match" work.

Attraction is a hard-to-capture element—a slippery component. Not only is it generated by unique personal preferences, but it's also influenced by constantly changing circumstances in the young woman's world. Back to my cell-phone example, the day could come when I would need more protection than the lovely peacock could provide. Say, if I started taking care of my two-year-old grandson on a daily basis. Then that phone-in-the-toilet thing would influence my choice. Life circumstances would change my attraction, and I would go for the waterproof overcoat.

Attraction Triggers

What triggers the attraction? Several scenarios. When events in a young woman's life force a problem or need to the surface, she looks for a woman who has been there and can show her a way to successfully navigate the situation. When she finds her own resources depleted, she is naturally attracted to someone who "gets" her situation and appears willing to help. She senses when another woman can be the resource she needs and naturally moves toward her. "I really do think you are drawn to certain people. I think the way you end up finding someone is through attraction," offered one research participant. Attraction creates the movement needed to start a comfortable relationship. When we attempt to predict attraction in others, we aim at a moving target and the process gets complicated. On the other hand, when we let natural attraction do the work, the process remains simple. Although each may need training first (we provide resources in the Appendices), mentor and mentee simply find each other.

Recently, my (Barbara) friend commented in a conversation with a group of young women that she was not raised in a Christian home. A short time later one of the women approached her and asked if they could meet for coffee. "You mentioned that you were raised in an unbelieving home. I was too and I would like to talk to you about that." The young woman observed that this trusted older woman managed to overcome the same obstacles she was struggling to overcome. The young woman longed for this in her own life, and that longing drew her to that particular woman. The older woman was approachable, available, and willing to use her experience to encourage another. A mutual attraction came into play, and this mentoring relationship was off and running with a click. When a young woman senses a click, her soul naturally opens and learns. Instead of an awkward situation, a vibrant connection launches the relationship.

Another attraction trigger revolves around gift mix and skill development. I (Sue) mentor younger women who observe me leading a ministry or teaching the Bible and say, "She's doing what I believe God wants me to do one day. I want to hear her story and learn from her." But not all future leaders and teachers ask me to breakfast. Some of them find another woman's leadership or teaching style more to their liking. I know this because years ago, I led a team of six volunteer Bible study teachers for a parachurch women's study. We taught round-robin style in six different Bible classes, and I wanted to learn which teacher was most effective.

I surveyed hundreds of women to learn that each teacher had her own special group of followers. To them, she was the best teacher, and they looked forward to her teaching more than the others because it "clicked" for them. They felt that she understood them and taught the way they learned. They enjoyed a special from-a-distance bond with her, and many could not explain why. God's marvelous creativity reveals itself in those natural attractions that jump-start thriving mentoring relationships. I'm never offended when a budding teacher chooses another teacher as her mentor. God makes us all different so that we can walk alongside the particular women who are drawn to us. No one can make this decision for another. But we can enlighten both older and younger women about the intricacies of thriving mentoring connections so they can make informed choices for themselves.

U-TURNS AHEAD

Mentees in the Driver's Seat

From our research and experience, we believe that older women must graciously release the mentor selection process and place it in the hands of the young women. They must be free to drive the mentoring process themselves, usually choosing their own mentors. You could even say we need a complete U-turn. Think of it this way: aren't we women known for our willingness to ask directions and turn around when we are going the wrong way? We need to apply this same wisdom to the mentoring process when a change of direction puts us on the right road.

Although older women can still initiate, young women become the driving force behind mentor selection. Lindsey, age 25, says, "I'm a firm believer that it's the mentee's job to find her mentor. I hate that it has come to where it has to be matched. That is just so unnatural."

But can we trust young women with this process? Will they choose wisely? We believe they will as the Holy Spirit guides them and as older women create environments where natural organic mentoring flourishes. More about that later.

Once we've made the necessary U-turn in our thinking about mentor selection, we'll head in the right direction. But we also need to rethink other aspects of the mentoring process where U-turns are in order.

It's about Life Change, not Information Dump

Many Moderns are also off course in their idea of what mentoring is all about. Too often we older mentors tend to think of mentoring as the transfer of knowledge from one woman to another. Certainly knowledge has its place in mentoring, but mentoring is more than teaching. In their book *Spiritual Mentoring: A Guide for Seeking and Giving Direction*, Keith

Anderson and Randy Reese suggest that mentoring ultimately fulfills the mentee's deep longing for spiritual navigation:

> There is a yearning, however, that isn't satisfied by the normal fare of personal study, prayer and worship. It is a desire for more, a "more" that is impossible to define or explicate; it is a longing to know the richness of "the deeper life" or "mature faith" or "spiritual power." There are times we may simply try to increase our devotional disciplines to satisfy our longing by reading more but discover that the longing remains unsatisfied. At other times we turn to the latest technologies, books, tapes or conferences hoping to satisfy the longing for more, but to no avail. We come to the realization we are not meant to make this journey solo.[6]

Mentoring is an opportunity to stretch and grow *with* another person, and the focus of mentoring needs to turn in this direction. Reflective thought, a larger perspective, deeper understanding, and openness of heart are all goals on the journey. When desires such as these stir a young woman's heart, usually the work of the Holy Spirit, we can trust her to seek a mentor.

The Focus Is on the Young Woman

In the early 1900s an aged English scholar, Baron Friedrich von Hugel, joyfully accepted the task of mentoring his adult niece. As he embarked on this mission, the Baron was keenly aware of the tendency of mentors to try to grow another in their own mold. "Souls are never dittos," he warned. Instead of creating another person like himself, the baron labored to expand and grow his niece's perspectives, personal gifts, and love for Christ. He urged those who mentor to pull their agenda from the process as soon as possible and instead discern how to develop their particular mentee.[7] In other words, mentoring is not primarily about the transfer of the mentor's knowledge, talent, or perspective; it's about facilitating the mentee's growth.

---

6   Keith R. Anderson and Randy D. Reese, *Spiritual Mentoring: A Guide for Seeking and Giving Direction* (Downers Grove, IL: InterVarsity Press, 1999), 18.
7   Baron Friedrich von Hugel, *Letters From Baron Friedrich von Hugel to a Niece,* ed. Gwendolen Green (Chicago: Henry Regnery Company, 1955), 36.

In the past we made mentoring about the mentor. The mentoring spotlight focused on her wisdom, talent, and godly behavior. If we look at mentoring as a stage play, the mentor would traditionally be cast in the starring role. The mentee was the understudy, a less experienced actress with a small part. She sat at the mentor's feet to learn her ways. Unfortunately, all too often in this situation, the mentee is asked to become a "ditto."

Anderson and Reese champion a new approach. They encourage mentors to "Probe your motivation. . . . Mentoring is not about you; it is about the other. If there is a desire to instruct and tutor another in the ways that you have found useful, perhaps it is time to think again. Mentoring is not about telling. It is about listening—to the Holy Spirit and to the life of the other."[8]

This approach swings the spotlight from mentor to mentee. The mentor steps out of the spotlight and places the mentee in the primary role. The mentee's life situation and learning needs drive the relationship, not the mentor's wisdom. This shift in emphasis changes the ethos of the relationship, which becomes more like a greenhouse focused on the one who needs care and tending.

A postmodern woman typically has a strong sense of individuality and does not consider herself a receptacle to be filled, makeover candidate, or potential ditto. But she does desire an experienced guide to help her respond to God's presence in her daily life. Instead of occupying an elevated place where she pours out knowledge, the mentor comes alongside to guide, counsel, encourage, and support the mentee as she learns to journey with Christ. Times of instruction, guidance, and wisdom will certainly be a part of this process, but mentoring is primarily about the needs, goals, and desires of the one being mentored. Mentor and mentee move away from a teacher/student relationship and walk together as companions engaged in the process of spiritual transformation.

The Mentor's New Role

If we step out of the spotlight, how has our role changed in the relationship? We may not be the focus, but we are indispensable as the experienced guide

---

8   Anderson and Reese, *Spiritual Mentoring*, 28.

invited to join the mentee on her spiritual journey. Long ago Augustine, an esteemed theologian of the early church, remarked, "No one can walk without a guide."[9] For centuries spiritual guidance has been considered an essential part of Christian growth. Stepping into the role of guide doesn't mean we are perfect people; it means that we are familiar with the path ahead and the possible pitfalls along the way. We accompany the new traveler through unknown territory, point out safe routes, warn of dangerous detours, offer helpful information, and apply first aid if necessary. Our new role is to become the experienced guide escorting our beloved charge on the unique path God designs for her.

Young women prefer mentors to function as caring guides. "I want to talk to someone who's a little bit further along on the path. That's a huge thing, just hearing from somebody who's done it. I'd like to hear her wisdom since I face that situation as well." An experienced woman's larger perspective is intensely interesting and helpful to a young woman.

We hear that collective sigh of relief. Many of us are quite happy to exit the mentor spotlight. We squirmed under that light, feeling unqualified. We don't know all the answers, haven't always behaved wisely, and are still engaged in the learning process ourselves; however, we *have* journeyed with Christ and learned some things along the way. Furthermore, we *can* comfortably focus on a mentee's journey and serve as companion and guide.

The shift from wisdom dispenser to guide is a welcome change for many of us. It lightens the load previously placed on mentors and reduces the intimidation factor. The "wisdom myth" convinces far too many of us that we are not wise enough to mentor. Meanwhile struggling young women try to figure out life by themselves.

It's Simply about Coffee

Now that the selection process is turned around and the mentee is free to select a mentor according to her needs, how does she connect with a mentor? We must not forget that the Holy Spirit is active in the process. He knows our needs and loves to respond with life-giving guidance (John 14:16–17).

---

9   Kenneth Leech, *Soul Friend: An Invitation to Spiritual Direction* (San Francisco: Harper, 1977), 41.

Prayer undergirds the pairing process and that must continue. God's essential hand guides in any mentoring initiative, and we encourage both mentor and mentee to pray for direction as they seek mentoring relationships.

We believe that, in addition to prayer, personal needs and life circumstances will cause a young woman to move toward a mentor. Natural attraction helps her find the right person at the right time. An organic mentoring relationship typically starts with an informal invitation to meet, usually initiated by the younger woman. "I was wondering if you could meet me for coffee? I would love your input on a situation." The invitation is as simple as that. Over coffee, lunch, or another informal setting, the mentee brings up a matter she would like to discuss, sometimes right away, or a question may emerge as conversation progresses. Maybe she needs advice on a dating relationship, an unruly child, or a career move, or she may be simply drawn to know more about a woman she admires. This meeting might be the first layer of an ongoing friendship or a one-time conversation that meets the mentee's immediate need. It's an organic process that develops naturally according to the mentee's interests. This approach feels safe and comfortable to young women.

Although it's a simple act, the way a mentee approaches us makes a difference. If she asks, "Will you be my mentor?" or "Will you mentor me?" she may unknowingly put us in an awkward position, and she may get a deer-in-the-headlights response. Our minds immediately envision endless meetings, pouring out wisdom we don't have, responsibility for another's spiritual development, and lots of time. Our brains frantically send out "preserve your life" signals, so we politely decline and assure the young woman that it's nothing personal. We just have too much going on at the moment.

Recently I (Barbara) received a distress call from Jody, the wife of a young college professor. One of his students enthusiastically asked Jody to "pour into her life." Overwhelmed by this request, Jody asked me, "How do I tell this student no?" A busy wife, mother, part-time employee, and church volunteer, she was convinced she didn't have time to pour into anybody. "Could you meet this girl for coffee periodically?" I asked. Yes, Jody thought that was definitely doable. With this different perspective, she was able to say yes instead of no, but the student's approach nearly sunk the relationship before it started.

The phrase "Will you be my mentor?" can burden an invitation with expectations that scare many of us off, but we find an invitation for coffee easy to accept. We believe older women are more receptive if young women avoid the word *mentor*.

If you receive what feels like an overwhelming invitation, consider the positive side: this young woman holds great respect for you. A wide-open opportunity for godly influence is at your doorstep. To scale back what might be unrealistic expectations, you could say something like, "I am honored by your invitation. Let's have coffee." When you talk, suggest the two of you meet periodically, which is probably her preference too. We teach young women effective ways to initiate a mentoring relationship in Appendix B.

The Dance

Some young women may lack the confidence to initiate a mentoring relationship, even to invite an older woman to a simple coffee outing. For them, the possibility of rejection isn't worth the risk, so they continue their lonely walk, without the guidance for which they yearn. Can we ever initiate the relationship? Yes, we mentors may sense the attraction first, and if we do, we may initiate the first contact. The Apostle Paul chose men to mentor as he traveled and planted churches. When he heard believers speak highly of a young man in Lystra, his interest was piqued. Paul later invited this young man, Timothy, to travel with him. Since Timothy submitted to circumcision and left his home for a rigorous journey, we can safely assume he felt a strong attraction to Paul as a mentor (Acts 16:1–4).

If a mentor senses that a click may be present but the mentee lacks the courage to pursue the relationship, we may need to offer some encouragement. Many young women respond enthusiastically to a mentor's invitation. I (Barbara) was blessed by such a situation. I was only seven years old when one of my mother's friends took a shine to me. A typical middle child, I believed nobody noticed me, but this childless matron was an exception. Delight danced in her eyes as we talked. My parents noticed the special connection and advised me to call her *Aunt Ann*, but I missed the subtle distinction and called her *Ann Ann*. My heart still lights up when I think of my overnights with Ann Ann. I don't know what drew her to spend time with me. I only know that on those coveted days I was an only child, my depleted little soul drinking in the attention and love. God may work first in a mentor's heart, drawing her to a woman who needs her. In a less orchestrated approach, the Spirit is free to work in either direction.

If we mentors sense a click may be present, we might take the first step by inviting the next generation woman to spend a little time with us, just to see if our hunch is correct. But then we place the pursuit back in the mentee's hands. We must never force the relationship. If we've initiated a connection, we've opened the door, and it's up to her to reciprocate or not. Don't be hurt if she doesn't respond or if she responds weeks or months later. Her timetable may be different from ours. Whether she accepts our overture or declines is not a measure of our worth as a godly woman. The compulsory click is either evident or it's not, and forcing a relationship seldom ends well.

Guard your attitude and words during a mentee's invitation. Just like a young man asking for a first date, some young women feel overwhelmed and awkward inviting someone they respect to spend time with them. You'll hear apologetic comments interspersed in the invitation, if they muster the courage to speak to you at all. Words like, "I know you are really busy. I'm sure you don't have time for this. I won't take up too much of your time." They place their tender hearts in your hands, and your response will either crush them or send them soaring. If you know that God is not guiding you to mentor this young woman, let her down gently, possibly over that initial coffee. But after spending time with her, you may find God convicting you to invest in her after all. If not, make sure she realizes you are not rejecting her personally.

Finding healthy mentoring relationships, for both mentor and mentee, resembles a dance. Each one takes steps toward or away from the other, as each discerns if this "match" is God's idea. Ultimately, the mentee must take the lead, even if she's shy and awkward. The relationship must meet the needs in *her* life, although the mentor can influence that decision, much like a responsive dance partner.

Be Ready!

Mentor, are you ready to respond to a young woman's invitation? If you turn down her invitation, she may think twice about ever approaching a mentor again. One young woman complained, "If you want a mentor, you have to take some kind of initiative or it just won't happen. But that means you have to put yourself out there, and that's not fun." Another added, "It's the mentee's job to pursue the mentor, but *we need to know* we can pursue them." Be aware that many young women perceive that older women are reluctant to invest in them. "Sometimes I feel like you don't want to, or you are too scared, or have insecurities about it. I wish there was more desire among women my mom's age to mentor us." Mentors who radiate acceptance, desire, and availability encourage young women and build their confidence to approach a mentor.

Although the mentee choses her mentor, Barbara's research discovered that mentees appreciate their mentor's occasional text or email saying something like, "I was thinking about you today. How are you?" Mentees often respond warmly with words like, "So glad to hear from you! It's been too long. Can you meet this week?" After your relationship is established, don't hesitate to show you care.

Multiple Mentors

The organic mentoring experience works best in a fluid environment. Some young women want a deep relationship with only one woman, while some desire input from several. Free them up to pursue various options.

Recently when flying, I (Barbara) rummaged through my stowed baggage and pulled out a mentoring book I hoped to read. The nineteen-year-old college student next to me found my book interesting and a lively conversation ensued. As we talked she expressed a strong desire to be mentored. When I asked her how she would choose a mentor, she responded that she would like many mentors. In her mind one mentor couldn't teach her all she wanted to learn, and it was natural for different mentors to be part of her growth process. This young woman pictured herself surrounded by a community of mentors.

Traditionally, we tend to think of mentoring as one mentor committed to one mentee for a specific period of time. But for many Postmoderns, one size does not fit all, and this structure won't work for them. Many young women prefer to customize their mentoring experience to accommodate changing situations. They may desire a one-on-one committed experience or prefer something less intense. A group mentoring experience with two or three friends may be their preference. A fluid environment requires flexibility and the availability of a number of mentoring options.

Many young women prefer to move among mentors, instead of talking with only one mentor, according to their circumstances, feeling constricted if tied to only one. In her book *Divine Secrets of Mentoring: Spiritual Growth Through Friendship*, Carol Brazo believes mentoring is most effective when mentors share the load:

> There are myriad ways in which we are mentored and in which we mentor. Mentoring is a kaleidoscope, a constantly changing field of color and wonder. It is not a linear path on which one chooses one guide and faithfully imitates. Mentoring and being mentored are full of faces and circumstances and discovery. Mentoring is a rich tapestry woven by a community of generous souls."[10]

Betsy, a gifted young woman whom I (Sue) mentor occasionally, expressed her need for multiple mentors this way: "I have different mentors that I seek out at different times in my life. If I have a question about my Bible teaching ministry, I come to you. If I have a question about another part of my life, I go to that mentor. I feel so blessed to have a number of mentors in my life."

We mentors may need to rethink our mentoring assumptions. If a young woman seeks time with several mentors, she's saying that she has different learning goals and wants to tap several sources. The postmodern world is full of many choices and different resource options, and Postmoderns feel natural moving among them.

A mentee's choice to move among mentors tempts some of us to conclude we are deficient in some way. That's faulty thinking. Move away from the idea that one mentor meets all a mentee's needs. Different types of relationships and a network of "generous souls" create more dynamic opportunities for her development. Rejoice and remember, mentoring isn't about you.

A New Focus for Everyone's Benefit

Good news—effective mentoring remains in great demand. But when we listen to young women's voices, we also hear bad news. Our practices of blind

---

10 Brazo, *Divine Secrets of Mentoring*, 17.

pairing, mentor focus, and a one-size-fits-all approach feel strange enough to repel them. They desire a simpler, more organic approach that welcomes their active participation. We need a change in focus to win them back. We enter their world when we make a U-turn. We let young women choose their mentor, facilitate a start that works for them, focus on their growth, take up the role of guide, and provide multiple mentoring opportunities.

The *great news* is these changes work to our advantage too. They make mentoring tasks simpler and more appealing to *both* mentors and mentees. An organic approach that allows relationships to develop on their own greatly reduces the structure-heavy feel. When you get used to the idea, you'll love the reduced workload. Organic mentoring benefits us all!

My mentor now, we have not clearly stated that it's a mentor/mentee relationship. It is a relationship that only the Lord could have put together. We found out that my mentor taught my mom the Bible the week or two before she died. My mentor invited me to a coffee shop one day to get to know one another better. Out of that invitation we have kept meeting at the same coffee shop. It is an informal/ organic kind of arrangement where we catch up on what is going on in each other's lives. We both encourage and learn from each other.

It feels more like a relationship if we can call or text each other when something is going on and not just meet at a regular scheduled appointment. I don't want to set a time with a therapist, but rather a friend. At the same time it is good for the mentor to check in on the mentee and hold them accountable. I think it is good to have the mentor send a message and just ask how they are doing with certain things. Don't leave the meeting times up to the mentee all the time. Plus, it's encouraging when someone wants to meet with me and not always because I'm calling them with a problem.

Stephanie, age 31

I know this book is geared toward older women BUT as a "postmodern" I was reading and thinking, "Wow this really IS how I like to find a mentor." I never saw the idea of initial attraction or clicking put into a concise explanation BUT that really is how my generation makes friends and in turn finds mentors.

Caroline, age 25

I hadn't realized that mentor matches were usually viewed by the women running mentoring programs as God-ordained, or at least valid and binding because they've been prayed over. The problem I have with this, though, is that it implies that the young women have no access to what the Holy Spirit is saying in the process—like we are waiting for the word from on high about what God has said. I know the process is well-meaning, but it puts the mentee in the position of almost a child, who doesn't have enough knowledge or experience to know what she needs. I think younger women just reject the idea that God wouldn't speak to them, too, in the whole process.

Kristin, age 32

CHAPTER 5

A New Commitment: Natural and Organic

If you require precision, order, sequential progression and careful forward motion, then you will be sorely disappointed, for spiritual mentoring is messy because life is messy, disorderly and random.

Keith Anderson and Randy Reese[1]

A mentoring relationship will survive on its own merits. If the mentoring partner is eager, coachable, and serious about learning, he or she will make it a priority to meet with the mentor.

David Stoddard[2]

You never want a mentorship to become obligatory. You want it to be desired because you are not going to learn if it is an obligation.

Berkley, age 23

"Mom, I brought you something," my (Barbara) daughter Juliet announced as she entered the kitchen where I was emptying the dishwasher. She plopped a gallon jug of dark liquid on the counter for my inspection. Glancing at the label I caught words like "juice," "compost,"

---

1   Keith R. Anderson and Randy Reese. *Spiritual Mentoring: A Guide for Seeking and Giving Direction* (Downers Grove, IL: IVP Books, 1999), 28.

2   David Stoddard, *The Heart of Mentoring: Ten Proven Principles for Developing People to Their Full Potential* (Colorado Springs: NavPress, 2009), 54.

and "garlic." I couldn't imagine how those words would ever fit together, but I took a closer look. "It smells like maple syrup," I remarked, still trying to figure out what I was supposed to do with the jug. "Yeah," she nodded, "it has molasses in it. It's an all-natural product with a whole mixture of things that will keep the bugs off your fruit trees and feed the tree at the same time."

Gardening along the humid Texas Gulf Coast is an all-out battle against an incredible variety of bugs, so I am usually willing to try out a new weapon, but really, organic syrup? When it comes to bugs chewing on my plants, I want *effective*. To be honest, I doubt this natural remedy is strong enough to do the job, but I give it a try. Later as I pour the mixture into my sprayer and drench my garden, I have an unexpected urge for pancakes.

Juliet's research on organic gardening led to the discovery of this organic pest control. While I have gardened for many years, Juliet is a beginner. She's a busy mom with four young children, and this is her first opportunity in a long while for an outside activity that doesn't involve pushing a swing or retrieving a dirt encrusted foreign object from a toddler's mouth. Her garden is located in a sunny patch of ground along the side of her house. She located untreated timber and built boxes to contain the dirt. She brought in organic soil and filled the boxes with a variety of organic plants. She feeds a nearby compost bin with organic scraps so the soil can be replenished with organic matter. She uses only organic products to feed and care for the plants.

Her organic urge thrusts me into unfamiliar territory. As I said, I value effective results in my garden and never thought molasses and garlic would get me there. So how did Juliet adopt this approach to gardening? She's a typical suburban gal with minivan and gym membership, she's a school volunteer, and she enrolls her kids in Tae Kwon Do—not exactly "granola." Yet, she is convinced naturally grown food is the best option for her family, and this conviction leads her to garden differently than I do. Anxious to see if this new molasses concoction works in my garden, I make careful daily inspections looking for leaf damage, cobwebs, and tiny sap-sucking insects, but find none. I am forced to reconsider; maybe this organic remedy works after all.

An Influential Movement

The organic movement began in Europe in the early twentieth century when a small group of farmers determined that man-made fertilizers produced deficient plants and began using only natural products to grow their crops. Most people considered this approach an eccentric fad. Eventually, in the 1970s, scientists discovered the unintended effects of chemical pesticides, and farming methods came under intense scrutiny. A push back against modern scientific practices erupted, and a return to natural agricultural methods gained traction.

Today the organic approach is a widespread movement, heralded largely by Postmoderns. Young moms concerned about their children's nutrition go out of their way to find organic options. Sue's daughter pays a dairy farmer to deliver fresh milk in glass bottles to her porch once a week. Many postmodern health and fitness experts recommend natural products for optimal physiological performance. Most grocery stores now offer organic products on prime shelf space, while specialty whole-food stores appear in more and more neighborhoods. Additional products such as cosmetics, shampoos, fabrics, and household cleaners tout their organic ingredients and find a significant clientele. Large corporations noted the popularity of the green movement and today invest billions of dollars to meet the surge in demand for organic products.

More Than Food

The organic movement started as a means to produce natural food but eventually grew into a belief system, one that is embraced by many next generation people. Organic elements shape their values and lifestyles in many ways. This belief system leads young people to a simpler, more natural and authentic way of life. It moves away from outside control, artificial ingredients, and synthetic products.

When we understand that the organic belief system also extends to the way Postmoderns relate to others, we begin to *get* them. Their relationships unfold naturally according to their own timetables. When we talked candidly with young women in our research, they all wished the mentoring process could be more "organic." When they look at the way we traditionally structure mentoring, they don't see organic. They see layers of additives that make the process feel unnatural.

IMPACT ON MENTORING

Organic Scheduling

"Organic!" exclaimed a mentor, "I am beginning to hate that word." Her obvious frustration grew from several conversations with young women. In her opinion, this "organic thing" was throwing up roadblocks to effective mentoring. "If everything is organic, how do we ever get anything done?" she frowned. That's a good question. Those of us new to organic might think that it means we abandon structure, organization, or direction, but that's wrong.

The organic movement values natural products and methods; however, it is not without intentionality. Organic farmers prepare fields, plant crops in specific locations, and add products to their plants to manage insect damage and weeds and promote the overall health of the plants. An organic method still requires tending; it is simply carried out in a way that assists natural processes. Like the organic farmer who continues to oversee and manage her crop, young women do not resist all structure, just too much structure, or what they perceive as erroneous structure. But locating the fine line between natural and overly structured is enough to make many older mentors a little crazy.

If you were mentored in the traditional method, you probably scheduled a weekly meeting and showed up on time. Both of you believed regularly scheduled meetings were necessary if you were to benefit from the relationship. But the constant refrain we hear from Postmoderns is that regular mentoring schedules don't work for them. An up-front commitment to a yearlong program that involves weekly contact is enough to send many young women packing. In their eyes, this seems like rigid micromanagement, and mentoring feels more like a forced task than a relationship. They say things like, "I don't want something that requires a huge time commitment. I want something laid back that fits my busy schedule."

Those who embrace an organic way of life prefer a mentoring experience that feeds and grows them naturally, instead of according to a timetable. "I want my mentoring relationship to have a family feel. I want to connect with my mentor at important times or when I have something to talk about," explained Emma, age 25. Is it possible an organic approach is strong enough to get the job done?

We believe effective mentoring can be both intentional *and* organic, but intentional no longer means yearlong commitments and weekly schedules. An organic approach lays the calendar aside and focuses on developing quality relationships. Commitment is still a part of the process, but we can relax and let it unfold naturally. Rather than checking off a weekly meeting, we need to think big picture. How is the relationship developing? Are we there for one another when needs arise? What is the quality of the time we spend together? We can be quite intentional about creating a quality organic experience and discover, to our surprise, that an organic approach works.

Term Limits

Mentoring programs often ask mentor and mentee to commit to a relationship for a specific period of time, and all participants begin and end at the same time. Some of us older mentors like this schedule because a fixed calendar keeps our life tidy and measures progress. When we launch a new mentoring year, we are excited about the possibilities. When the mentoring term comes to a close, a satisfying sense of accomplishment follows. After a brief rest we're ready to fill in the calendar again. But a conversation with our younger sisters reveals that they view the requirement to meet with someone week after week for months as an impossible obligation. What feels like accomplishment to us feels like a burden to them and isn't popular.

Young women tell us the lower the required commitment, the better it works for them. An organic approach allows the mentee to decide how long the journey with a mentor will last, and she won't have a feel for this immediately. One woman finds a brief walk gets her to the destination, while another may want a companion who will walk with her for years. One research respondent explained, "If this is about living life, it is wrong to set a time standard. When should a book end? Read it as slow or fast as you want. Read it again if you want to. Mentoring shouldn't be for six or twelve months. This is a free fall, and I think it will come with natural time clocks."

The length of a relationship depends on a number of different factors, such as how long it takes for mentor and mentee to develop rapport, the learning goals of the mentee, the type of relationship the women seek, and the movement of the Holy Spirit. Mentoring is a subjective endeavor that will grow and develop according to the characteristics of the people involved. Determining when it is complete is a decision best made by those people. Many Postmoderns desire mentors who will be an ongoing part of their lives. They may see this mentor often, or there may be years-long gaps in their connection, but this woman will always be considered a go-to person when needs arise. Let go of the need to control these relationships and simply let the Spirit lead.

Teachable Moments Drive the Schedule

If we eliminate yearly contracts, relax weekly schedules, and create a flexible environment, what motivates a mentor and mentee to meet? Remember how the mentoring click came from the combination of trust and attraction? These two elements give us a head start and usually provide the motivation necessary to initiate and sustain a relationship. Once mentor and mentee make contact and establish a relationship, teachable moments in the mentee's life and valuable insight from the mentor will keep them going.

Driven by Her Need

Young women seek a mentor because they are motivated to learn and grow. As children we were required to learn regardless of our motivation. Those older and wiser saw to it that we learned the basic skills necessary to function in society. But when we become adults, the learning process changes. Adults learn what they want to learn, not what someone else thinks they need to learn.[3] Educator Laurent Daloz remarks that pushing an adult to learn is about as effective as trying to push a chain uphill.[4] It's slow going without internal motivation.

---

3   Peter Senge, *The Fifth Discipline: The Art and Practice of the Learning Organization* (New York: Doubleday, 1994), 345.
4   Laurent A. Daloz, *Mentor: Guiding the Journey of Adult Learners* (San Francisco: Jossey-Bass, 1999), 182.

I (Sue) felt responsible to teach my children to pick up after themselves and help around the house. When they were in grade school, I employed fun charts and reward and demerit systems to motivate them to make their beds, clean their rooms, set the table, and a variety of other simple chores, all designed to shape their character and work ethic. I wish I could say that they tackled these chores with gusto, whistling a tune, and thanking me for the privilege. If you are a mother, you know I'd be lying. Excuses, bad attitudes, whining. I couldn't get them to change the toilet paper roll without complaining.

The teen years weren't much better, until my daughters were chosen to join a team of camp counselors at Pine Cove, the Christian camp they loved growing up. We visited one weekend to meet their teammates and see how they were faring. I hardly recognized them. Their camp duties included washing and changing sheets in the cabins, scouring the bathrooms, serving meals to hundreds of people, and scraping and washing piles of dishes in the kitchen. I watched them tackle these mundane tasks with enthusiasm. Who were these young women? They were fervent in their efforts because they were serving the Lord. They were part of a team with a purpose and they loved doing their part. Sadly, when they returned home, they were still blind to the reality that the toilet paper roll needed replacing when they used the last piece of toilet paper, and they couldn't remember how to load a dishwasher. The power of internal motivation.

Adult motivation often kicks in when a problem needs solving. The strongest learning experiences originate from real need that pushes us to engage situations and seek solutions. Problems also motivate us to turn to mentors who might help us find that solution. In Chapter 4 we recommend mentors step out of the spotlight and focus instead on the mentee and the problems she wishes to solve. This new way to mentor moves away from schedules and facilitates an unscripted process where the mentee takes a more active role. She is now in the driver's seat and develops the mentoring relationship according to her needs.

"It would be ideal if I had free rein to contact my mentor when I wanted to," responded Sara, age 28. "I need stuff at different times. I can't just schedule this out." Sara wants to learn, but she also needs an opportunity flexible enough to respond to the moments when she is ready to learn.

Flexible scheduling releases more of the process to the Holy Spirit as we depend on Him to bring a mentee's internal needs to the surface at the appropriate time. As Paul Stanley and Robert Clinton point out, "Most people need personal guidance often throughout their lifetime, but not on a fixed schedule."[5] Mentoring is a dynamic process that involves an issue in the mentee's life, the movement of the Holy Spirit, and the mentor's insight. The times when a young woman "needs stuff" prompts her to meet with a mentor.

Right Help at the Right Time

Since people are complex individuals with different needs and levels of motivation, the frequency of meetings will vary from woman to woman. Women differ in their ability to process and apply spiritual truth, and spiritual growth is often slower than we wish in our results-oriented culture. Older mentors may be tempted to think little is accomplished when the schedule is sporadic, but our research indicates that's not true. "Our meetings are not scheduled, but every time we get together, I get something out of our time," reported Brittany. When a mentor guides a young woman with the right help at the right time, it's transformational. The mentee learns a new perspective that she is able put into practice immediately, and it's often life changing.

I (Barbara) find mentoring most effective when a mentee comes to me with a question generated by a current life situation. It might be solving a relational problem, handling a crisis, seeking input for a decision, recovering from a divorce, or learning how to write a Bible study. Often the young woman remarks, "Thanks! This has been so helpful." Our conversation was beneficial because she came ready to hear another perspective and solve a problem.

Often one conversation isn't enough and we schedule another time to meet and continue the discussion, or sometimes a single encounter meets her need. Young women in my life know that I'm available to mentor, and they contact me when a teachable moment surfaces. They probably don't

---

5   Paul D. Stanley and J. Robert Clinton, *Connecting: The Mentoring Relationships You Need to Succeed In Life* (Colorado Springs: NavPress, 1992), 66.

see it as a "teachable moment;" it's just a time when they need to process a life event. But because they come with something *they* want to learn, the experience is valuable, and they are motivated to contact me again when another need arises.

The last thing we want is a mentee who shows up because the meeting was on the schedule and she felt obligated to come. Then we find ourselves pushing a chain uphill and mentoring turns into a burden. If the time together is valuable, she'll be back for more.

By now you may be thinking, this feels strange. Why should we, the older women, accommodate younger women, when *organic* feels so unnatural to us? Jesus shows us why.

MENTOR WITH THE SAME MIND-SET AS JESUS

Jerusalem's stone streets lay silent and dark, echoing an eerie premonition of the tragic day ahead. The gravity of Jesus' mission pressed in. With the Twelve around him, He reclined beside a table littered with remnants of lamb, unleavened bread, vegetables, vinegar, and wine. The traditional Passover meal, celebrated one last time with His disciples, was wrapping up. A somber mood hung in the room as Jesus passed around the bread and wine, giving birth to a new covenantal ordinance that His followers would practice in remembrance of Him for millennia. More questions than answers stirred in the disciples' heads. Jesus had only a few hours left to burn one last memory into their hearts before He returned to God.

"He got up from the meal, took off his outer clothing, and wrapped a towel around his waist. After that, he poured water into a basin and began to wash his disciples' feet, drying them with the towel that was wrapped around him" (John 13:4–5). Jesus took on the task usually carried out by a homeowner's lowest servant as He tenderly removed the dirt caked between His disciples' toes and washed the odor from their calloused feet. His disciples resisted. They knew this was backward. The duty of devoted disciples was to honor their master by washing *His* feet.

"'Do you understand what I have done for you?' he asked them. 'You call me "Teacher" and "Lord," and rightly so, for that is what I am. Now that I, your Lord and Teacher, have washed your feet, you also should wash one another's feet. I have set you an example that you should do as I have done for you. Very truly I tell you, no servant is greater than his master, nor is a messenger greater than the one who sent him. Now that you know these things, you will be blessed if you do them" (John 13:12–17). An object lesson impossible to forget.

Later the Apostle Paul described the significance of Jesus' behavior this way, "Do nothing out of selfish ambition or vain conceit. Rather, in humility value others above yourselves, not looking to your own interests but each of you to the interests of the others. In your relationships with one another, have the same mindset as Christ Jesus" (Phil. 2:3–5). For those who appreciate brevity, Paul summarizes the message in Romans 12:10, "Be devoted to one another in love. Honor one another above yourselves." On the night before Jesus went to the cross, He embodied Paul's words and showed us how He wants us to relate to the younger women He calls us to mentor.

Who Is the Servant?

When we peer into the historical context of this incredible Passover night, an important custom surfaces. When guests entered a dwelling to celebrate the Passover, shoes were removed and feet washed by a servant before they headed to the table. Someone was missing at this Passover meal—the servant. When the disciples arrived, apparently no servant was on duty, so they removed their shoes and proceeded to the table with dirty feet. Not one of them was motivated to take up the washing chore. Later, the almighty Son of God took on the role of the servant in the room. Jesus' words, "I have set you an example," must have burrowed deeply into the disciples' minds and hearts while eyes sought the floor. That night, Jesus taught His beloved disciples through His own example that they were to serve others, and then He left for the cross.

"Have the same mindset as Christ Jesus." "Honor one another above yourselves." Words that are hard to shake off. When older mentors incorporate flexibility into mentoring, they become the servant in the room. They value others above themselves. They wash feet. We are sometimes convinced the younger ones should respect our ways and wash our feet. In some ways that may be appropriate. But how will young women learn to be servants if we don't show them? When we're the servants in the room, they see how it is done. We teach them to wash feet as we wash theirs. Isn't that the way

Jesus did it? Older mentors who take up the role of servant make deep impressions on young women's minds. The mentor's ways become memorable, an example burned into a young heart. Let the serving start with us!

Who Loves First?

Jesus not only served His disciples but loved them deeply. They gave Him many frustrating, eye-rolling moments, but He loved them and they knew it. If you want to mentor the next generation, you must love them. You must love them through frustrating, eye-rolling moments—like when they want *flexible* and *organic*. Postmoderns have an uncanny ability to detect phoniness and they know when someone pretends to love them. However, genuine love on the part of a mentor is magnetic, and when young women sense it, they can't stay away. Let the love start with us.

Older mentors who love young women deeply and take up the role of servant make flexible and organic happen. But let's not forget that Jesus promised that those who serve as He did will be blessed. "There truly is no greater joy than giving your life away to others," writes David Stoddard, "People matter more than things, goals, and achievements. And the greatest satisfaction in life comes, I believe, when you give your life away to something that really matters."[6] Joy and satisfaction flood our own hearts when we see young women grounded in Jesus and growing in faith and servanthood—a win-win situation.

Stretch Your Availability

Think about meeting mentees at times you might consider inconvenient. Could you occasionally meet on a weeknight or Saturday? We know a highly respected mentor in her eighties who meets at 6 AM with a small group of young women. We find that if God wants these relationships to thrive, He works out the timing, and if we are flexible, He makes up for the time invested. "It's hard to connect with a lot of older women," Dawn confided, "because I work during the day, and they tell me they have to be home with their husbands at night, or they are doing things with their grandchildren on the weekends." If we truly want to serve young women, we need to meet them when they are available.

---

6   Ibid., 39.

PROVIDE ORGANIC OPTIONS

Our research reveals that young women also desire options in their mentoring relationships. We mentors tend to think of mentoring as a formal one-on-one commitment where one person agrees to develop another, but that's only one way to mentor. Different forms work for different people. For example, the classic one-on-one relationship may work well for introverts who generally find inner reflection natural, but might be less optimal for extroverts who find high-energy connections more attractive.

Open the door to an organic approach, and step outside the traditional mentoring box. Create a mentoring menu with more natural choices and opportunities tailored to the desires of your particular group of young women. Listen to their needs, ideas, situations, and problems and create options that work for them. You might consider the following options:

Formal Mentoring

Formal mentoring stands at one end of the spectrum and often occurs in business or education, sometimes in the form of an internship or apprenticeship. Often a young woman seeks this type of mentoring relationship when she admires the skill or maturity of another woman and wants to absorb that skill or way of life. She may initiate a formal agreement. This one-on-one approach often consists of a long-term relationship, regular meetings, formalized goals for the mentee, and high personal investment. This type of mentoring requires a greater time commitment on the part of both women and looks the most like a traditional approach, with regular meetings and spoken commitment. However, to work today it must still have the organic start we talk about.

Realistically, mature mentors who can handle this type of investment are few and hard to find. If this is what a mentee seeks, it may be a lengthy quest. But if we broaden our view of mentoring, we find other more available options.

Informal Mentoring

Informal mentoring occupies the middle of the spectrum and is easier to find. Young women who seek informal mentoring are usually looking for timely advice or guidance whenever they request it. They often choose informal settings to meet: a coffeehouse, restaurant, or any convenient location that simply offers a place to talk.

When I (Barbara) mentor, I usually meet the mentee at the nearest coffee shop. Already an ingrained part of her culture, the coffee shop provides the leisurely and nonthreatening atmosphere where conversation over a latte is natural. It doesn't feel like "mentoring," it feels like meeting for coffee, and that's the feel I'm going for—coffee and informal conversation.

With informal mentoring, the mentee usually wants to discuss a personal situation. She needs a listening ear and another perspective. She doesn't want to commit to a formal agreement to keep meeting, although both women may be open to additional meetings. If they do meet another time, it's scheduled when the mentee wants to talk again. Informal mentoring requires less time and is less intimidating for both, and because there is no fixed schedule, one mentor can usually mentor several young women at the same time. This mentoring-on-demand arrangement can be tailored to suit the young woman's situation, and our research indicates that most postmodern women prefer this approach. "There is so much structure in life," lamented Kasey, "I want something informal where you can share your heart, share what's going on, or work on what's been going on in your life. That works better for me." Informal mentoring creates the organic feel many young women desire.

Passive Mentoring

Passive mentoring stands at the other end of the mentoring spectrum. Passive mentoring takes place when a woman reads a relevant book, listens to a speaker, attends a conference, or engages in serendipitous conversations with mature women. As seminary professors, we enjoy multiple opportunities to mentor students before and after class, walking in the halls, standing in the parking lot, exchanging quick emails about assignments, or greeting across the campus. These opportunities for passive mentoring afford brief moments to ask questions that help us "take the pulse" of our students and respond with appropriate words. They also help us discern whether a longer time together might be advantageous.

From these contacts, women pick up helpful life principles that can stimulate their growth. I (Sue) tell my students that profound life-changing exchanges occur at these divine intersections and we should ask God to use us even in these short simple moments together. Wherever we are, whatever we do during our day, we can reflect Christ through passive mentoring opportunities. However, when a personal mentor is available for an extended time, young women often receive insight that moves them forward faster and deeper.

Group Mentoring

The foreword of Jana Sundene's book *Shaping the Journey of Emerging Adults*, coauthored with Richard Dunn, was written by four young women she mentored as a group for over eight years. They wrote,

> For the four of us, the presence of mentors like Jana has anchored us in the fast moving and sometimes threatening course of our lives. When we have faced vast uncertainty and the dreaded need to "rise to the occasion" of adulthood, the voice of reassurance from an established adult has countered our disorientation with a stability that is founded in Christ. When the waters around us have changed too rapidly or at times too slowly, the men and women who have journeyed beside us have taught us not only to wait upon the Lord with expectancy but also to recognize his presence in the heart of the chaos. When a myriad of voices have drawn us into confusion, we have benefited from the perspective of mentors who have challenged us to attend to the one Voice who speaks through his Spirit, his Word, and his community.[7]

The four women were in their early twenties when Jana began meeting with them regularly. They tout her wisdom, a willingness to share from her own life experience, and her presence as their equal—all qualities that strengthened their group and helped them through difficult transition years.

Group mentoring can be another form of effective mentoring. Some groups, like Jana's, delve deep into life issues, utilizing peer mentoring and

---

7   Richard R. Dunn and Jana L Sundene, *Shaping the Journey of Emerging Adults: Life-Giving Rhythms for Spiritual Transformation* (Downer's Grove, IL: InterVarsity Press, 2012), 10.

group accountability as powerful tools in women's lives. Other small groups are designed to meet the short-term needs of several women, sometimes focusing on a skill or particular interest. For example, cooking, budgeting, parenting, writing for publication, career guidance, marriage, infertility, prayer, miscarriage, couponing, sewing, etc. Rich possibilities for group mentoring exist. Many times the young women suggest a topic or designate a particular mentor for group mentoring.

Group mentoring is also a great opportunity for young women to mentor their peers, or even older women. The next generation is proficient in some things we older women struggle to master, and their expertise can help us grow. If you want to be mentored in organic gardening, building a website, smart phone shortcuts, or use of social media, seek out a young woman. These groups are different from classes or teaching in that they are deliberately kept small and based on the active participation of the mentees. Shy women often find group mentoring a safe place to start, and extroverts may find this option more attractive than one-on-one.

SUMMARY

A young woman's preference for organic opportunities with built-in flexibility may seem like lack of commitment to us older mentors. We worry that these sporadic schedules lead to weak mentoring experiences. But what feels like weakness to older mentors feels refreshing to younger women. Release from prescribed schedules frees her to develop a natural relationship that comfortably fits her lifestyle and particular needs. If time with a mentor adds value to her life, commitment follows and the relationship survives on its own merits.

Someone once said, "Don't feel bad if people remember you only when they need you. Feel privileged that you are like a candle that comes to their mind when there is darkness." A mentor who builds into a young woman's life according to her schedule is like that candle. She is available light, remembered when there is a need. When it comes to mentoring schedules, internal need is a potent motivator, and we can trust it to bring women together.

I've been blessed with a wonderful mentor, who I met through a program at my church. We were asked to meet weekly for a semester. That intentional meeting time those first few months helped us develop a friendship that I cherish. However, there were definitely times that I was swamped with work and other commitments that made the weekly meeting seem like just another item on my to-do list. We decided to continue meeting on our own, as our schedules allow, separately from the program, and I'm so thankful. My mentor has become my friend—one that I can call or text at any time, about anything. We pray for each other's families and talk about what we've each been studying or reading. I'm thankful for the organized program that brought us together, but the friendship that we have developed over the past two years goes way beyond any regularly scheduled meeting.

Autumn, age 29

A potential mentor should realize that she may not even know she is mentoring a younger woman. I recently spent time with an older woman in our church to discuss some things about a particular study we were having at our church. Really, I just wanted to know what we were studying and express my concern about some of the book choices they had made in the past. She responded well to my concerns, and then in the course of talking, we got onto an unrelated topic—the older woman began to talk openly about mistakes she felt she had made in the spiritual guidance of her children. I have small kids and wonder almost every day how to most effectively guide them to Christ. This woman didn't give me a program, or really even any "answers," but I have chewed over her comments on what she would do differently for days. And I want to ask her more. Does she think she's my mentor? Probably not. But that day she did mentor me, and probably will in the future. She doesn't have a title of mentor, but it didn't make her any less effective for something that I wonder about.

Elisabeth, age 27

Term limits don't feel like a relationship if you put an "expiration date" on it and say I'm only going to commit to you for a year. This makes it hard for me to open up and trust the person. Life goes through seasons and you will know when you need to meet or not.

Stephanie, age 31

CHAPTER 6

A New Goal: Transformation Through Shared Experiences

Many Yers, used to the direction, drive, and support offered at school and at home, are floundering amidst a sea of choice, opportunity, and reality. . . . They need a broader context for action and decision-making, a sense of meaning and purpose.

Rebecca Huntley[1]

The notion of telling young women not to do things because the Bible says so just doesn't wash in this culture. Pre-adult women are looking for a real live person who can demonstrate the wisdom of biblical concepts from the story of their own life.

Earl Creps[2]

I want my mentor to tell me about her experiences, when she was in a similar struggle, and how she made decisions. It is just beneficial for me to see the Lord moving in her life.

LaKeisha, age 27

1   Rebecca Huntley, *The World According to Y: Inside the New Adult Generation* (Crows Nest, NSW, Australia: Allen & Unwin, 2006), 184–185.

2   Earl G. Creps, comment on "We Live in a Circus: The Culture of Pre-Adult Women," earlcreps.com blog, comment posted on May 11, 2009, http://www.earlcreps.com/article/we-live-in-a-circus-the-culture-of-pre-adult-women.

Satisfying warmth settled into my soul as I (Barbara)
packed up my Bible study notes after another evening discussing God's
Word with several bright, honest young women. For about eight weeks
we met to go through a book of the Bible. Discovery of biblical truth
both delighted and sobered us as we wrestled with the implications.
"Mission accomplished," I thought as I tucked the notes into my Bible,
"These women grasp the connection between biblical truth and how to
live." Maybe not.

Before I could make my exit one of the young women approached me
with a hopeful request, "Can you meet for coffee?" Later in the week, I
listened to her share what was *really* on her mind. Yes, insights from God's
Word interested her, but an unfulfilling job had derailed her spiritually, and
she didn't know how to get back on track. She wanted to know if I'd ever
experienced anything like this, and if so what did I do?

WHAT DOES THE BIBLE SAY?

I spent time regularly leading these women through God's Word, but this
young woman also needed help applying the Bible to her specific situation.
Our conversation over coffee was especially impactful in her life because we
were taking advantage of a teachable moment. My method moved from a
more formal school-like model to a more organic approach. Moses affirms
this approach in Deuteronomy 6:4–9, a familiar section known as the *Shema*.
Even today Jews memorize this text as little children.

Moses wrote this passage at a critical time in Jewish history. He had led
the Israelites out of slavery in Egypt and soon they would enter the Promised
Land. Just before he died, he taught them the *Shema*, parting words to a
beloved people that he had shepherded for forty years. Dying words are
important words. Although directed to parents to help them pass their faith
on to their children, they apply equally well to mentors today.

> *Hear (Shema), O Israel: The Lord our God, the Lord is one.*
> *Love the Lord your God with all your heart and with all your*
> *soul and with all your strength. These commandments that I*
> *give you today are to be on your hearts. Impress them on your*

children. Talk about them when you sit at home and when you walk along the road, when you lie down and when you get up. Tie them as symbols on your hands and bind them on your fore-heads. Write them on the doorframes of your houses and on your gates. (Deut. 6:4–9)

The Hebrew word used here for love *(Ahah)* speaks of a fiery, consuming passion for God that permeates all of life. We show our mentees that love when we take time to listen to their individual stories and concerns, helping them apply God's Word to their current situation. The word *impress (Shanan)* challenges us to make them hungry for God, to be involved in the process God is using to transform them. The verbs are all present tense, reminding us that these relationships are ongoing.

Moses paints pictures of people interacting naturally as they go through life together. He suggests we interact as we sit around at home enjoying a meal or taking a walk, before we rest at night, or as we greet one another in the morning. We see a Hebrew parent sharpening her child's spirituality by responding to the child's questions that come up during the day, through teachable moments as they live under one roof. Most of us won't live with our mentees, but we can adapt these methods to our mentoring.

We create informal connections that facilitate the important questions and insights that draw our mentees closer to God, giving them insight as to how to live for Him in their individual circumstances. The interaction is natural, casual, not structured like a school. Topics come up anytime, anywhere, in the midst of life. Unlike an academic or preachy approach, the tone takes on natural sharing.

Two different teaching models have flourished through the centuries: the Greek model and the Hebrew model. Our formal educational in-stitutions use a Greek model that works well for structured schooling. Students sit in classrooms and progress through levels of instruction as they prepare for careers and life. The Greek model was highly valued in the Modern era, the five-hundred-year period of history that ended around 1980, and it still has its place today. When we older women think about mentoring, many of us see the relationship taking on the flavor of the Greek model. We are the teacher and our mentee is the student. But that is not what younger women look for.

In a mentoring relationship, most young women are drawn to the Hebrew model, the model we observe in the *Shema*. Moses favored this biblical approach for transformational impact. Younger women look for older women who will include them in their daily routines, talk about current challenges over coffee, and be available, not according to some prearranged schedule, but when needs arise. No prep time required.

Moses encourages us to try this organic approach instead of formal lessons and preaching at our mentees. Furthermore, he tells us to "tie" our influence as "symbols on our hands and bind them on our foreheads." Your hands represent personal caring and touch. What will your mentees think about when they think of your hands? If you use your hands to communicate God's unconditional love and tenderness, God can use them to encourage and heal deep emotional and spiritual wounds. And what about our foreheads? Some Jews place tiny rolls of scripture in little boxes and literally tie them on their heads. We don't believe Moses is asking us to design a new form of headgear; instead this mandate refers to our minds and the minds of our mentees. As we sharpen one another's minds through stimulating conversation and life-on-life sharing, our minds become a tool God uses to help us walk by faith and understand Him better.

Finally, Moses tells us to "write them on the doorframes of your houses and on your gates." The doorframes probably represent our inner domain, our private spheres; the gates represent the outside, our public spheres. Mentees learn from us in both places. So go places together. Join together on tasks you need to accomplish anyway. Mesh these separate spheres when you can.

WHAT YOUNG WOMEN WANT TO LEARN

We often assume that our mentees want to learn what we wanted to learn the way we wanted to learn it. But that's a mistaken assumption. We were hungry for knowledge, but they dwell in an avalanche of easily accessible information. Their mentoring goals are not more information, but opportunities to process life with honest godly women.

A Different Question

> *I want an older woman who will draw me out, who will ask me questions and make me process the events of my life. She would say, "Wait—stop. Tell me more about that."*
>
> Alexis, age 30

In her eye-opening book *Shaping the Journey of Emerging Adults: Life-Giving Rhythms for Spiritual Transformation*, co-author Jana Sundene describes her first attempt at mentoring. "I was guilty of approaching her with an agenda—one that really didn't have much to do with her—rather than exploring her questions. . . . I was also serving a method. The discipleship book that was placed in my hands became *the way* to serve her. . . . it hung between us like a film that I could barely see her through, and our discussions fell flat."[3]

Like Jana, many older mentors choose to teach a Bible study or spiritual curriculum. We love curriculums because they simplify the mentoring process and show us what to do with our mentee. The material is easy to follow, provides a focus, and gives us that all-important feeling of accomplishment. Curriculums are often expertly crafted and full of valuable information, but frequently don't have much to do with a mentee's questions. She may gain new information but not know what to do with it.

I See You

The woman sobbed and buried her head in the crook between her husband's neck and shoulder during a scene from *The Joy Luck Club*. I (Sue) remember thinking that I'd never heard so much audible weeping from so many women during a film. Salty tears streamed down my cheeks too. The scene struck a deep chord in my soul, a yearning for the love of a mother who had so little to give. After the movie, we strangers, some still sniffling, encountered each other in the bathroom and bared our souls in an unusual but honest conversation for a public restroom. The power of story and film on display that night.

---

3   Richard R. Dunn and Jana L. Sundene, *Shaping the Journey of Emerging Adults: Life-Giving Rhythms for Spiritual Transformation* (Downers Grove, IL: InterVarsity Press, 2012), 79.

The movie chronicles the lives of five Chinese immigrant mothers and their American-raised daughters. Relationships writhe in misunderstandings due to cultural and generational gaps. These mothers love their daughters fiercely with the best intentions, but their high hopes often come across as impossible expectations that leave their wounded daughters feeling like failures.

The scene that caused all these tears centered around an exchange in the kitchen as mother Suyuan and daughter June clean up after a tense Chinese New Year's dinner. Mom has cooked her famous crab, all best quality except one with a damaged leg. To Suyuan this crab is no longer edible, worst quality, but more dinner guests attended than she expected, requiring her to include the damaged crab on the serving plate. As the plate made it rounds, June instinctively grabbed the crippled crab, leaving the best quality crabs for the other guests.

During dinner June and Waverly, lifelong friends and rivals, scrapped over a business issue. June felt humiliated when her own mother complimented Waverly by saying, "True, cannot teach style. June not sophisticate like you. Must be born this way."

Cleaning up in the kitchen, June confronts her mother by telling her how much those words stung, adding to her frustration that she had disappointed her mother throughout her whole life. Tearful, June accuses, "You never see what I really am." Her mother responds by honoring June above Waverly for taking the worst quality crab. "Only you try to take it. You took because you have best quality heart. You have style no one can teach. Must be born this way." Then she takes the face of her beloved daughter into her hands, looks deeply into her eyes, and declares, "I see you. I see you." For the first time June felt seen.

Young women today long to hear those words, "I see you. I see you." Many never have. Powerful, soothing, healing words straight from Jesus through you. Mentoring the next-generation requires a new goal. Instead of the transfer of prepackaged information that informs thinking, our goal is to "see" the mentee, to help her walk with God in a postmodern environment and discover the woman God created her to be. This is what most young women yearn to learn from us. Curriculum can be valuable, but unless it's introduced at the right time and in the right way it can "hang like film" between mentor and mentee.

Different Problems

Women in their twenties and thirties face opportunities and problems most of us never encountered. While we probably settled into marriage and career by our midtwenties, a postmodern woman typically finds this a time of instability during which she struggles with personal identity, independence from her parents, finances, morality, and faith.[4] At the same time seemingly endless possibilities call her to keep exploring the options out there.

As a result, confusion, stress, and anxiety rule many young lives. "We see so many in this generation living harassed and helpless, like sheep without a shepherd. . . . Emerging adults long for mentors who will provide navigational guidance as they face a changing societal landscape where values and markers are no longer clear."[5] Mentoring offers a place for reflective thought so crucial to spiritual growth and so difficult to grab in our fast-paced culture. The greatest need of many women in the next generation is a caring shepherd who "sees" her and offers guidance and stabilizing truth connected to her life.

Impact of the Self-Esteem Movement

My (Barbara) three children sat cross-legged on the floor, eyes glued to the TV. Calm settled over our living room as the gentle middle-aged man opened a door, put on a cardigan, greeted his "neighbors," and invited them into his neighborhood. I was grateful for the thirty-minute break that allowed me to address chores unhindered. Every weekday Mr. Rogers nurtured millions of young minds and taught children to believe in themselves because they were special and valuable. This message was heard again at school, where teachers labored to cultivate a child's positive self-image by offering large doses of affirmation for being a unique individual. It even wafted from our car radio as Christian musicians told children they were special from head to toe, and we all sang along.

The 1970s gave birth to the self-esteem movement. By the 1990s it was an entrenched part of American culture and self-fulfillment became a personal

---

4   Christian Smith, Kari Christoffersen, Hillary Davidson, and Patricia Snell Herzog, *Lost in Transition: The Dark Side of Emerging Adulthood* (New York: Oxford University Press, 2001), 15.

5   Dunn and Sundene, *Shaping the Journey of Emerging Adults*, 20–25.

right. Generational researcher Jean Twenge, a Postmodern herself, remarks, "We simply take it for granted that we should all feel good about ourselves, we are all special, and we all deserve to follow our dreams."[6] Self-esteem is a person's evaluation of her personal worth, and it's widely believed children with high self-esteem will be successful in life.[7] They are assured that if they believe in themselves they can be anything they want to be. As a result the majority of Millennials, our youngest mentees, are highly optimistic and believe they will do something great.[8] Not just worthwhile, but *great*. Sounds wonderful, right? We should all feel this way about ourselves.

Not so fast. Twenge's research also shows the self-esteem movement can cause problems when children grow up. Too often the fallen world does not treat them as special, they discover they can't really be anything they want to be, and their work is ordinary. "GenMe'ers are also often woefully unprepared for what we encounter in the 'real world' of the marketplace."[9] Self-esteem actually has little to do with success in life. People with high opinions of themselves still make destructive choices and wind up in dead-end situations.[10]

We now have a generation of young people with high self-esteem but nagging inner suspicions that they are actually deficient. Many hold high expectations for their lives but struggle to make them happen. How does a young mom cope when her life of diapers and runny noses is anything but great? Failure to meet optimistic goals often leaves behind confusion, disappointment, and anxiety, and too many feel like failures before they are thirty.

We don't need to return to the days when parents feared that praise would spoil their children. Constant criticism destroys tender souls, as

---

6 Twenge, *Generation Me*, 49.
7 Abraham H. Maslow, *Motivation and Personality*, 3rd ed. (New York: Harper & Row, 1970).
8 Ariel Schwartz, "Fast Company: Millennials Genuinely Think They Can Change the World and Their Communities," Telefonica Global Millennial Survey, June 27, 2013. http://www.survey.telephonica.com/globalreport/.
9 Twenge, *Generation Me,* 130.
10 Roy F. Baumeister and John Tierney, *Willpower: Rediscovering the Greatest Human Strength* (London: Penguin, 2011), 187–213. Nicholas Emler, "The Cost and Causes of Low Self-Esteem," *Youth Studies Australia* Vol:21, Issue:3 (September 2002): 45–48.

many older women know from experience; however, excess praise without substance can also be damaging. The peril of the pendulum. Often next-generation women need help to rethink their expectations for life. A shift from an optimistic me-centered vision to a God-centered perspective may help them comprehend God's purpose for their lives and restore biblical balance and inner peace. Here a mentor can make all the difference. When life is processed together, we can help a young woman identify unrealistic goals that stall her spiritually, provide God-centered perspectives, temper self-esteem with self-control, and encourage her to follow God-given dreams. This happens when we "see" our mentee and the deep needs in her life.

HOW YOUNG WOMEN WANT TO LEARN

If we don't focus on prepackaged materials, what do mentor and mentee talk about? When our goal is to see the mentee, it's natural to talk about life—events, whether good or bad, and the questions that arise from them. Discussing life experiences is frequently how a young woman wants to learn from her mentor.

Connect It for Her

> *I like to hear about things in her life. I like to hear about how God has moved and worked in her life. It reminds me that if she lived through something, so will I.*
>
> Brianna, age 26

Truth reached through evidence and logic holds little interest for many postmodern women; however, they find truth connected to real-life situations compelling. Stories from a mentor's life often make this vital connection to truth. For example, if a mentor mentions that faith overcomes fear, the mentee's response is likely to be, "Okay, but how do you do that? Have you ever done that? How did it happen?" She essentially says, "Tell me a story about how this truth works in real life. I want to know how to get where you are." If the mentor relates a time she was gripped with fear but managed to calm down through faith in God's presence and provision, the mentee finds the mentor's hands-on experience convincing.

When you share a personal experience you tell a memorable story. Stories have always been an effective way to engage the mind and are fundamental to the way humans learn. When we tell stories we discover common ground. Experiences take on depth and meaning, and relational bonds form. When you relate a particular time God was present, the younger woman can often see similarities to her situation and a possible new response. "When I hear her stories, I start to see things in my life and how the Lord might be moving," confided a young woman.

However, those of us steeped in the analytical method may not be so sure about stories. We tend to see a close tie between correct information and godly living, and often think the best way to learn truth is through analytical study. This has its place, but it may not deliver the same impact on Postmoderns that it had on you. Presenting truth through sharing life stories is often a difficult concept for us to grasp. Not only that, it feels uncomfortable and maybe even unbiblical. "I don't think we should talk about ourselves," countered one older mentor, "I think we should talk about the Lord. I feel uncomfortable talking about myself."

A close look at the Bible reveals that storytelling is the format used most frequently. In book after book, God speaks through stories as the real-life adventures of an amazing variety of characters stir our minds and move our hearts. When we see their struggles, similar struggles in our lives surface. Faith maintained in hardship increases our courage. Those who fail and experience restoration give us hope. A story often triggers something deep within, a connection jumps to life, and transformational understanding takes place. "Stories have a way of sneaking past the defenses of the heart."[11]

Jesus frequently harnessed the power of stories to teach truth and stop people in their unthinking tracks. Near the end of His ministry, He told a story about a vineyard leased to a group of tenant farmers (Luke 20:9–19). The vineyard's owner rightfully expected a portion of the harvest and sent representatives to collect; however, the tenant farmers beat, shamed, and ex-

---

11 Reg Grant and John Reed, *Telling Stories to Touch the Heart* (Eugene, OR: Wipf and Stock, 1990), 7.

pelled his servants empty-handed. In one last attempt to deal with the tenants fairly, the owner sent his son to collect what was owed. This time the tenants used the opportunity to kill the heir so the property would default to them. At this point in the story, Jesus paused and asked the crowd to consider what the owner of the vineyard would do next. Since many in the crowd were farmers, he allowed the truth in the story to sink in. He then revealed the end of the story: the owner would return, kill the tenants, and give the vineyard to others. The story delivered a powerful punch that was not possible through a logical conversation and unnerved a group of religious leaders standing nearby. "The teachers of the law and the chief priests looked for a way to arrest him immediately, because they knew he had spoken this parable against them." Although Jesus never mentioned these men, the story revealed their own hardened hearts, and they angrily responded with a plot to kill Him.

Truth comes to life when framed in a story. Vivid stories in the Bible teach us who we are, who God is, and principles of truth that enable us to draw near to Him and live better. They also possess unique ability to build bridges across generational divides. "What's helpful is the mentor sharing her story," mentioned one mentee. "I hear her story and think, 'Oh, I want to know more about that.'"

We aren't suggesting mentor and mentee simply swap stories when they meet. Storytelling is only one component of mentoring. But most Postmoderns do learn truth best when it is revealed through stories that connect with life, reveal the truth, and enable real-world application. Understand that you have more to offer than prepackaged lessons from a book. Your life is a rich resource that can make a difference in the journey of a young woman.

Transparency

When I say I struggled to get up this week, struggled to open my Bible, I want her to say, "You know what, sometimes I do too." I don't want a perfect woman who always says, "Well, you should have done this." I want someone completely transparent who can say, "I didn't either—life is messed up, I didn't either."

Tara, age 24

To successfully mentor next generation women, a mentor must show herself to be a real person with real problems. We are not talking about full disclosure with all your dirty laundry hanging out. We're talking about humility that allows us to admit we are not perfect. This requirement will challenge some of us to the core of our being. Just as Postmoderns were raised in the self-esteem movement, we were raised in the "Be a Good Role Model" movement and transparency just feels wrong. Our background leads us to believe our mistakes will lessen our influence or affect someone negatively.

Craig Groeschel, pastor and author of *Alter Ego: Becoming Who God Says You Are*, addresses our bent: "I was trained in seminary not to be transparent. They called it 'guarding the pastor's mystique.' That was one of the most dangerous teachings that the older generation passed along. It was wrong. If you are not being transparent, you are not going to reach this generation. You have to be authentic."[12] The idea of a mystique may appeal to us, but it won't get us anywhere with our younger sisters. "When I meet with a mentor," revealed a postmodern woman, "I think, 'Okay, is this mentor going to let her guard down and let me see the real person?'" She wants a person, not a mystique.

The Apostle Paul, probably the most respected man in Christianity, was quick to admit his deficiencies. The church in Rome heard about his battle with coveting (Rom. 7:7–8). He told believers in Corinth that when he arrived in their city he was weak, fearful, and trembling (1 Cor. 2:1–3). When he reached Macedonia he acknowledged outward conflict and inward fear (2 Cor. 7:5). While encouraging his mentee Timothy, he mentioned his sinful past as a blasphemer, persecutor, and violent aggressor. In perhaps his most vulnerable moment, he described a painful condition he was not able to overcome (2 Cor. 12:1–10). Paul saw himself as a fellow struggler and one who needed Christ's mercy the most (1 Tim. 1:13–16).

Transparency is often difficult for Christians. We rightfully expect each other to live up to God's standards. But sadly, too often our failures bring rejection, which tempts us to hide our deficiencies, problems, and pain. One frustrated older woman described the situation this way:

---

12 Craig Goreschel, "When Church Becomes a Pastor's Idol," *Leadership Journal* (Spring 2013): 85.

I think there is a huge lack of transparency in the church. We can't be real. I found my best Titus 2 ministry began when my eldest child flaked out on us and became a prodigal. Instead of hiding it, I decided I would be transparent about our struggles. Women flocked to me because, as painful as it was, I chose to be real. If we are all perfect mothers, perfect lovers, and perfect churchgoers, we create a big fallacy where we leave no room for the Holy Spirit to work, and we operate by a system that only appears biblical. I think the younger generation sees the holes in this, calls it bunk, and does their own thing. And I can't blame them.

Dealing with our sin is part of the spiritual growth process. Most of us are willing to admit we sin. But it's hard for some of us to admit *exactly how* we fail—to talk about particulars. When we guard our "mentor's mystique," hide specific faults, and disclose only positive characteristics, young women find it difficult to relate to us. Remember, these are "keep it real" people.

When we admit we don't have it all together, we simply agree with what the Bible teaches: we are all fallen people who desperately need God's grace and redemptive power. Author Carol Brazo describes how God uses transparency:

> None of us is whole. None of us reached adulthood without broken places in our lives. We live in a fallen world and all of us yearn for the wholeness we were created to reflect. It is a gift of enormous measure to share our brokenness with others. Sharing allows others to see areas in which God is at work. It allows them into the Healer's office to watch the miracle begin. And it reassures us the miracle we seek can be found at his feet.[13]

Instead of losing credibility, you gain stronger standing when you share honestly about your life. Let young women see your problems and how you work with the Spirit to overcome them. Let them see how God

---

13 Carol Brazo, *Divine Secrets of Mentoring: Spiritual Growth Through Friendship* (Downers Grove, IL: InterVarsity Press, 2004), 79.

forgives sin, and how the everyday process of redemption and restoration takes place. Give her hope for recovery from her own mistakes. Allow her to see how God uses your experiences to strengthen and conform you to the image of Christ. Your faith experiences are a window through which she can see the work of God and biblical truths become more than ideas; they take on skin.

When we speak honestly about our imperfections, insecurities, and frustrations, we create a comfortable place where our mentee can do the same. Weary of living in a culture that values achievement and success, many Postmoderns long for a relationship where they can relax and be honest.

You will determine the level of transparency in the relationship. In response to Sue's blog post on mentoring, one woman commented:

> I've spent years looking for a mentor-type Christian woman and this is where I get stuck. I can't imagine a more experienced woman who wouldn't judge me for the sin struggles I have, because I can't imagine any of these women *really* sinning. When we pray for each other we pray for health, jobs, and safe travels. No one asks for prayer for recovery from a past abortion or affair. And, I think to bring about change it's going to take our leaders raising the bar.

More and more we hear from women who are desperate for real help. If you guard your mentor mystique, shallowness will characterize the relationship and the young woman is likely to exit. Appropriate disclosure of your thoughts, feelings, and actions during difficult times enriches the relationship and creates a substantial experience for the mentee.

MUTUALITY AND PARTNERSHIP

On the Same Level

> *A mentor is someone who guides you, answers your questions, and helps you out. And I can do the same for her.*
> Tamika, age 27

In the past a mentor sat at a higher level than her mentee. For many of us this hierarchy seems natural. Older and wiser equals "above." But this idea hasn't translated to the next generation. In the postmodern world, hierarchies don't make sense because each person's contribution is equally valuable. Young women see mentoring as friendship between equals. If we assume the elevated position of "answer woman," our mentee is likely to lose interest. For those of us who feel insufficient to mentor, this is good news. We can step down and simply relate as women following Jesus.

But we older women must often work to get to a place of mutuality. We may gladly give up the "answer woman" role, but still face temptation to assume the role of the mentee's mother. Because we can see a little further down the road, we frequently want to tell her what to do. This attitude on our part can quickly shut down the relationship. Young women participating in our research indicated they did not want another mother, and they did not want to be told what to do.

Preference for mutuality also means many next generation women expect a reciprocal learning experience. Just as she learns from you, she assumes you will learn from her. Although this idea might sound crazy, we think she happens to be right on this one. God designed the biblical community as a connected system, where all parts make contributions to each other. Instead of gifts flowing in only one direction—from greater to lesser—they flow from all directions. When you "see" your mentee, her gifts can enhance your life, and you benefit from the relationship as much as she does. "While Margaret is further along in her spiritual walk, she has learned from me," recounted a next generation woman. "I work with the homeless and introduced her to that ministry. She loves it and comes with me when she can."

Seasoned mentor Lesa Engelthaler confesses, "One thing I discovered about mentoring is that I often benefit from what my mentees have to say." One evening Lesa went straight from work to meet a mentee. A job-related frustration preoccupied her thoughts as they conversed over dinner. "Then something happened that was so God-like. Melissa is about ten years my junior, and she's also fairly new in her faith. Yet her profession as director of human resources makes her my 'senior' in the work world. Melissa asked me about the situation I was facing. When I told her, then out of her mouth flowed the most amazing managerial wisdom, which was exactly what I needed to hear."[14]

Our next generation women are exceptionally gifted in certain areas. Tap into this resource. If she is good at something, ask her to teach you. Become the mentee on occasion. Let her see you have growth areas just like she does. An atmosphere where both women learn builds a rewarding relationship that draws them together again and again.

MENTORING WITH INTENTIONALITY

It's More Than Hanging Out

> *She cared for me but she did not hold back speaking truth into my life when she saw that I had wrong thinking.*
>
> Emily, age 31

It's easy to confuse mentoring and friendship. Friendships are essential connections important to our sense of well-being. Women need friends. Times with friends bring laughter, listening ears, and encouragement. As friends browse the sale racks, their conversation may lead to an important question and an opportunity for biblical guidance. But the conversation often goes no deeper than bargains and the latest with kids. Friendly advice may be offered, but rarely are friends intentional about moving us toward maturity in Christ.

A pitfall with an organic approach is that mentoring relationships can get stuck on the friendship level. The women spend time together, tell each other about their lives, and encourage each other, but there is no spiritual movement. We mentioned previously that young women learn best through sharing life experiences, but mentoring is more than telling someone about your life. Mentoring is a relationship with a purpose. Without purpose the relationship can meander aimlessly, becoming little more than friends "hanging out."

Mentoring is more than friendship or giving advice. Our purpose is to help young women follow Christ and be transformed into His image. Intentionality in the relationship allows us to move in this direction.

---

14 Lesa Engelthaler, "Good Mentoring," *Leadership Journal* (Summer 2006):86.

Listen with a Purpose

Mentoring that appeals to postmodern women starts with careful listening. Her world of connection-through-technology creates hunger for a patient, wise listener. When busy schedules rule the day, listening may seem like a waste of time. On the contrary, listening is a powerful mentoring tool. When you listen carefully to your mentee, trust is built and she feels accepted, valued, and understood. You begin to *see* her, and her heart begins to open to you. A mentee is unlikely to receive your input until she feels heard and understood. "I joined a mentoring program but dropped out after two months," revealed a young woman. "My mentor kept telling me what to do, but she didn't even know me."

Develop Quality Conversation

An intentional mentor facilitates quality conversations. As you listen with purpose, eventually guide the conversation beyond what happened and who did what. Ask good questions that bring out what is going on inside your mentee. Questions like, What do you dislike about this situation? What do you dislike about yourself in this situation? What are you confused or upset about? Where do you need help? How do you want to change? What do you sense God wants you to do? Make no assumptions and give *no advice* at this point; only listen.

Good questions help you listen to your mentee's heart and discern where she is spiritually. After she answers, summarize what you heard and let her verify the accuracy so both of you grasp her situation. When the mentee hears her own thinking, she begins to see the problem, and the door opens for spiritual growth. Good questions lead her to reflect, something she probably seldom has time to do, allowing her to process her life in light of God's truth. Quality conversation takes the relationship beneath the surface and creates the depth young women crave. Her needs bubble to the surface. When this dynamic is present, she feels *seen.*

Discern Her Spiritual Situation

Spiritual mentoring needs to be both organic and organized. Coming from Auckland, New Zealand, which is called the "City

of Sails," I see the organized elements (such as showing up in
each other's lives, listening "fiercely," and asking great questions)
as hoisting the sails so that the organic elements (the wind of the
Spirit, in an attitude of daily dependence) can hit our sails and take
us to places in our relationship that we would never have dreamed.

Rowland Forman[15]

Organic mentoring may be natural but isn't without effort. As the mentor
listens she works hard to discern the young woman's place on her journey
with Jesus. To do this you must listen to the mentee, the Spirit, and yourself—all at the same time. Now, that takes serious mental and spiritual effort.

As you listen to the young woman, be alert for unbiblical thinking, sinful
or unwise behavior, harmful habits, strengths, weaknesses, gifts, knowledge
of the Bible, her understanding of God. Is this mentee just starting the
journey, or has she traveled the road for a while? What experiences with
God does she bring with her? Listen for what the Spirit reveals and how
He might direct the conversation. God is the one who causes growth, and
He has opinions about the life of your mentee. How is He moving? You are
there to help her hear and respond to God's presence and activity in her life.

Listen to your own thoughts as well. What obstacles in her life do you
observe? What comes to you from Scripture? Is there a similar experience
in your life you can relate? Mentoring is a dynamic interaction between
listening and discerning. This has been referred to as "wholly listening,
holy listening, and holy seeing."[16] Mastery of this skill enables you to bring
life-giving truth to your mentee and comes with practice over time. Give
yourself grace and depend completely on God to work through you in the
process. He will.

Use of Curriculum

As you and your mentee identify her needs, a book or Bible study
could be helpful. Most next generation women are open to a "study" if it

---

15 Rowland Forman, *The Lost Art of Lingering* (McKinney, TX: Confia Publishers,
    2013).
16 Anderson and Reese, *Spiritual Mentoring*, 13.

relates to their current need. If you don't know much about the subject, no problem; you can learn along with your mentee. Mutual learning creates the collaborative atmosphere she loves. Remember, you are not the answer woman. She chose you because she trusts you and wants to learn from your life, so relax. If a book is selected, be sure to discuss it together instead of "teaching" the material.

It is our opinion that mentoring should include biblical truth. God's Word is foundational for all of life and too many postmodern lives are untouched by it. Encourage your mentee to attend a strong Bible study to complement your influence in her life. We find that many young women already attend a Bible study and don't want more of the same in mentoring. Nevertheless, in the mentoring relationship they *are* open to exploring scripture that relates to their needs and growth goals.

Remember, the mentor is always responsible to bring God's perspective to the table. If your mentee is not in Bible study, you want to think about how to introduce God's Word into your relationship. If she has never done Bible study before, it may take some time for her to value God's Word and want to learn from it. Once your relationship is established, the two of you may decide to choose Bible study as a growth goal, and you can teach her how to study God's Word, or perhaps attend a Bible study together.

SUMMARY

Traditional approaches to mentoring led us to believe that study of pre-packaged material was the best way to grow a young woman. Our young women have voted and this is not their choice. Instead they want a mentor who listens to their lives. They hunger for truth presented in a believable format. They want to see firsthand how God works in a woman's life, how to know and obey God in a messed-up world. Shared life experiences give them opportunities to connect their lives with biblical truth. If we want to draw our young women back, relationships must switch from a teaching focus to a relational focus where shared experiences are prominent.

When you make it your goal to *see* your mentee and respond to *her* needs, both of you experience a rewarding relationship. She grows, you grow, and

An ideal mentor/mentee relationship would be very organic, natural and real. I would be fine going several weeks and not speaking to my mentor, or on the contrary, speaking three or four times in one week depending on my circumstances. I don't need a set schedule that makes it necessary to meet just for the sake of meeting. In a mentor I need someone to listen, offer insight, share her experiences, and just be willing to "do life" with me. I don't necessarily need a "Bible study" partner, which is often what Millennials get from older mentors. I enjoy spending time with an older woman who can be genuine and real with me, and not feel like she has to present a certain image of herself as the "wise older woman." I would be very interested to hear her failures and regrets, as well as her successes and accomplishments.

Sharon, age 32

Mentoring really is more like a guide type relationship than a sit at your feet and learn type relationship. There is a time and place for both, but for so many women (especially in an information saturated age) we can find all the information we could ever need BUT we can't find that heart to heart, person to person, direction and advice that we need without the influence of a mentor, a guide, essentially a friend.

Caroline, age 25

I struggle with self-esteem issues. I have three babies and one on the way and often wonder where I belong. I love my family more than anything but with some broken bridges in the past I'm not sure it's where I want to be. I would love to be mentored on how to succeed in my marriage and fall back in love with my title as a wife. I often feel stuck with not having a positive role model growing up. I am glad to know now that I'm not alone with these issues.

Kodi, age 25

CHAPTER 7

The New Community: Your Place to Connect

The best way to be formed in Christ is to sit among the elders, listen to their stories, break bread with them, and drink from the same cup, observing how these earlier generations of saints ran the race, fought the fight, and survived in grace.

James Frazier[1]

The old often save the young and the young save the old.

Mary Pipher[2]

God has woven community into everything—from himself, to the nation of Israel, to the church, and in the future. For some reason I had never seen it that way before, but it makes total sense!

Angela, age 36

If third-party pairing is out and organic relationships are in, how will mentor and mentee find each other? They often discover that natural fit or click in some kind of intergenerational gathering. When asked how

---

1 James Frazier, "All Generations of Saints at Worship," in *Across the Generations: Incorporating All Ages in Ministry: The Why and How,* ed. Vicky Goplin, Jeffery Nelson, Mark Gardner, and Eileen Zahn (Minneapolis: Augsburg Fortress, 2001), 56–63.
2 Mary Pipher, "The New Generation Gap," *USA Weekend,* March 19–21, 1999, 12.

she would find a mentor, twenty-five-year-old Amiee responded that she would identify a woman and say, "Hey, I like you. I like your life and how you live it. Can you teach me that?" But identifying that woman presupposes Amiee has opportunities to meet and observe older women. More of a challenge than you might think. Intergenerational gatherings are becoming harder and harder to find. In this chapter we'll discuss the current age-segregation trend and what to do if you want to mentor a next generation woman but are frustrated by lack of opportunities to connect.

It Really Does Take a Community

A solo mentor can serve as a lifeline for a younger woman, but the best environment for a Postmodern to grow strong in is a healthy intergenerational community with multiple mentors and role models, robust peer relationships, and sound Bible teaching. Sometimes these factors are available and sometimes they aren't. As a mentor, you can only do your part; however, sharing the load with others is best for your mentees. Guide her toward these resources when possible.

The root systems of the giant California redwood trees picture the strength and magnificence of healthy community. I (Sue) remember driving through the trunk of one of these immense trees as a child on family vacation. The canopy of redwoods spans some fifty miles, the tallest trees reaching more than 350 feet into the sky and twenty-two feet wide at their base. Imagine a natural city of thirty-five-story skyscrapers, their foundations decorated with ferns and ivies, and a kaleidoscope of wild flowers in spots where the sunlight streams through. Breathtakingly beautiful, some redwood trees were around during the Roman Empire. What I did not know until recently is the secret to their vitality and longevity.

The secret is their unusual root system. Unlike most large trees, they don't send down a taproot. Instead they grow a broad, shallow root system, their deepest roots only about five or six feet. But what they lack in depth, they make up for in width, as they spread thousands of tentacles as far as 150 feet out in every direction from the trunk. Their roots intermingle and even fuse with roots from other redwoods, creating a massive shared anchoring system that benefits everyone. They thrive in thick groves but without this combined strength they're vulnerable, easily toppled by the wind. Together however, many have weathered twenty-two centuries of whatever comes their way.

Solomon wrote, "A cord of three strands is not quickly broken" (Eccl. 4:12). Imagine cords of thousands of strands. Healthy faith communities who anchor their lives together in a love for God and one another provide redwood strength for emerging adults searching desperately for a place to put down roots. They yearn for multiple mentors who can nurture and guide them as they find their way in a dangerous and difficult world. Healthy communities foster mentors who work together to provide supernatural strength for floundering Postmoderns.

As I interact with young women, I hear them describe an overwhelming sense of disconnect. Even if they grew up in a strong family, many share that they are now "on their own," unsure of where they belong. Many faith communities don't seem to understand the postmodern generation, resulting in these young women experiencing a sense a detachment. School days provided natural communities, but now as they venture into first jobs and new cities, those natural communities have disappeared.

They describe this detachment with different words: feeling homeless, drowning, wandering, or sidelined. Although their lives may involve many online "friends," these shallow relationships leave them empty. They yearn to be part of something that matters and to do something significant with their lives. But many express inadequacy as they face life-altering decisions. Is God real? Is the Bible true? Have they chosen the right career? Should they get married? Are they enough? And so on. . . Connecting with life-giving mentors and a community that guides and cares can steer a young woman onto a path that leads somewhere instead of nowhere. But how will the mentor and mentee find one another if their community is age-segregated? They are certainly at a disadvantage.

The Problem

Communities that offer the most opportunities for mentoring relationships are intergenerational. What do we mean by the term *intergenerational*? To some, *intergenerational* means a community that includes several generations, but in reality that community may still be age-segregated. The singles, young marrieds, empty nesters, seniors, and other groups belong to the same large community, but they learn, worship, fellowship, and serve without ever crossing paths. They are segregated. They pass each other in the hall or worship service like ships in the night and don't know one another. A better term for this kind of community would be *multigenerational*.

When we use the term *intergenerational,* we mean that meaningful interaction occurs *between* these different generations. An intergenerational gathering might be a small group, Bible study, Sunday school class, social outing, mission trip, service opportunity, or an entire spiritual community where the lives of women of various ages and stages intersect enough for mentoring relationships to be birthed naturally.

Sadly, in recent years, more and more communities have organized themselves according to strict age boundaries, leaving people generally dissociated from anyone unlike themselves.

Holly Allen, co-author of *Intergenerational Christian Formation*, tells a story about a college student in her church who attended the funeral of a much-loved matriarch. A friend commented, "I didn't know you knew Mrs. Ellison." The college student replied, "Oh, I don't. I just wanted to come to a funeral. I've never been to one before. I've been coming to this church for a few months, and they have been praying for Mrs. Ellison ever since I've been coming, so I wanted to come. . . .You know, I've never been part of a church where there are old people who die. It changes the way you see life."[3] Everyone loses when women are denied the privilege of learning from those ahead and behind.

Reasons for age-segregation vary. Some communities organize this way out of convenience. Dealing with differences easily breeds conflict if Moderns and Postmoderns are not taught how to value, embrace, and honor one another. These tensions break out in families, at workplaces, on ministry staffs—wherever the generations come together to accomplish a task or learn something new. Yet the benefits of working through differences outweigh any negatives. As we join hands and hearts, our lives reap rich benefits and we grow up.

---

3   Holly Catterton Allen and Christine Lawton Ross, *Intergenerational Christian Formation* (Downers Grove, IL: InterVarsity Press, 2012), 31–32.

> Churches who value their young and their old will have to deal with clashing perspectives, which may slow things down, make decisions harder to come by, force compromise on difficult matters, and automatically elevate the value of relationship over that of task. But when generations collide, the ensuing conflict reminds everyone, Church is not just about me. Who knew the church could be the cure to narcissism?
>
> Chad Hall[4]

Others have given in to the demands of the groups, and we understand the tension. When I (Sue) led a ministry with women, I set up the Bible study's small groups as intergenerational only. Remember, that means the groups would intentionally include women of different ages. Some of the young mothers let me know their dissatisfaction by leaving our study and setting up their own Bible studies in homes. The quality of the different home studies varied, and the following year, many young mothers wanted to return to our study, but only if they could be with their friends.

Our women's ministry leadership team decided to accommodate their request by offering choices. Young mothers could join a group with their peers, but two seasoned mothers would serve as leaders. Everyone liked the compromise. In time however, I noticed a curious trend. Many of the young mothers looked around at the intergenerational groups and decided for themselves that they were missing a valuable experience. So the next year they signed up for a group composed of women of all ages and from all walks of life. Sometimes ministry is like herding cats, messy and ambivalent. But God asks leaders to herd them nonetheless.

Both age-specific groups and intergenerational groups have their purposes, but one huge downside of age-specific groups is the lack of potential mentoring connections. Unintended consequences follow leaders who fail to think through all the ramifications of this decision. If your community has erected tall walls between generations, it may be time to consider how

---

4   Chad Hall "*All in the Family* is Now *Grey's Anatomy*: Today's Segregation Is by Age," *Leadership Journal* 27 (Fall 2006):33

to scale those walls, at least sometimes, for the benefit of both older and younger folk who are missing the abundant blessings that relational connections afford.

> A great deal of America's social sickness comes from age segregation. If ten fourteen-year-olds are grouped together, they will form a *Lord of the Flies* culture with its competitiveness and meanness. But if ten people ages 2 to 80 are grouped together, they will fall into a natural age hierarchy that nurtures and teaches them all. For our own mental and societal health, we need to reconnect the age groups.
>
> Mary Pipher[5]

WHAT DOES THE BIBLE SAY?

The First Community

The concept of community began before creation in the Godhead: three distinct Persons, one essence and one purpose. God reveals Himself as a personal God who enjoys and pursues relationships. Whatever God touches has the marks of relationship. God is a "We," not a "Me." God's very nature models community for us, showing us the importance of interdependence.

When you become a Christian, you're not primarily adopting a set of abstract principles, although Christianity does adhere to truths and standards that proceed out of God's love. When you come to faith, you are falling in love with the Person of God, who exists as Father, Son and Holy Spirit.

The reality of God as Trinity is mysterious and has caused us no end of problems. Try explaining this concept to seekers. Vast amounts of paper and ink have been devoted to the task, and some of the ideas are helpful, but in the end the Trinity defies logic. But God doesn't care. He's communicating significant truth. He's telling us that to Him community is high value, and He wants it to be high value in our lives too.

We who live in the West usually think like Westerners, which can make us oblivious to what community really means. We are raised to value freedom

---

5   Pipher, "The New Generation Gap," 12.

and independence. But if we go to extremes and declare independence from God and one another, we hinder life in authentic community. People in biblical times naturally thought in terms of the group first, but we Westerners seldom do, which results in few of us really knowing what authentic biblical community looks like.

I (Sue) came to this realization when I was preparing a seminary course on small group ministry. As I read books and planned learning experiences, it dawned on me that although I valued community and wanted to see it lived out among God's people, I really didn't understand what biblical community was all about. I've intentionally tried to think more biblically since.

Community in the Garden

The first two chapters of the Bible, Genesis 1 and 2, picture a perfect community. God created Adam in His own image and enjoyed a rich relationship with him. Adam had everything he needed: meaningful work, beauty, nature, and most of all, face-to-face times with the Trinity, whatever that looked like. Wouldn't you love to have been there! But even that was incomplete, and God created another person, a woman, as man's companion, and for a time they rejoiced in their communion with God and each other. But then rebellion fractured community, and oneness morphed into separation between God, man, and woman. Life since the fall has been characterized by isolation and alienation, not God's ideal. God immediately set in motion a plan to redeem us individually, as well as a plan to restore corporate community. That plan is now in process.

Community in the Nation Israel

After the fall, God could have dealt with people as individuals, a logical approach from our perspective. Instead, He chose a special people, a community of folk that would experience a special relationship with Him, for the purpose of wooing the rest of the world to Him. In the Old Testament, a Jew's worst fate was exile from Israel. To be an Israelite meant one shared a strong corporate identity with fellow Jews. Even today, Judaism fosters an intense interrelatedness that is often missing in Christian congregations. My (Sue) family lived next door to a Jewish family for twenty-four years, and our children grew up together. These neighbors lacked a solid faith in

God, but they fervently celebrated every Jewish holiday within an intensely loyal Jewish community.

Jewish history explains these tight bonds today. The Roman Emperor Titus destroyed the second Jewish Temple and leveled Jerusalem in AD 70. As a result, the Jewish people fanned out into seventy different countries, yet they have maintained their Jewish connectedness for over two thousand years. Nothing short of miraculous! God still loves the Jewish people, and they are an important part of His eternal plan; however, as a nation they failed to woo the world to God, and so He set Israel aside and created another community for that purpose.

Community as the Church

Jesus left behind a new community that was formally birthed on the day of Pentecost (Acts 2). During His earthly ministry, Jesus used special words to describe this new kind of community when His mother and brothers were looking for Him.

> Then Jesus' mother and brothers arrived. Standing outside, they sent someone in to call him. A crowd was sitting around him, and they told him, "Your mother and brothers are outside looking for you."
>
> "Who are my mother and my brothers?" he asked.
>
> Then he looked at those seated in a circle around him and said, "Here are my mother and my brothers! Whoever does God's will is my brother and sister and mother." (Mark 3:31–35)

Jesus used family language to describe how believers should relate to each other. His church would be a close knit family of all ages. And notice that Jesus added the word *sisters* in the last verse. In a culture where women were often undervalued, Jesus made a special point of including women in this new kind of community.

During His earthly ministry Jesus established His own small group of mentees, the Twelve Apostles, and within that group, He was even closer to three, Peter, James, and John. Don't forget the band of women that followed along undergirding the work financially. As I look at Jesus' intentional inclusion of women over and over in the Gospels, I'm left believing that Jesus called women to join His special group of mentees for fireside chats from time to time. Listen to Jesus' last words before He went to the cross. First He prayed for His apostles and then He prayed for us.

> My prayer is not for them alone. I pray also for those who will believe in me through their message, that all of them may be one, Father, just as you are in me and I am in you. May they also be in us so that the world may believe that you have sent me. I have given them the glory that you gave me, that they may be one as we are one—I in them and you in me—so that they may be brought to complete unity. Then the world will know that you sent me and have loved them even as you have loved me. (John 17:20–23)

His last words are a call to sacred community, with the ultimate purpose of winning the lost. Jesus prayed that our communities would be so unified and full of love that they would woo the world. Authentic communities are a strong witnessing tool to Postmoderns who reject rationalism but value spiritual life. Jesus' mandate for unity compels us to flush out competition, cliquishness, and jealousy. When we do, our communities will correct distortions about Christianity heralded in the culture and serve as incubators for mentees who want to grow in Christ.

A look into New Testament letters continues to show us the priority of community. Many of these letters contain practical mandates that tell us how to live the Christian life. Most of these instructions contain plural pronouns in the Greek, but they look like singular pronouns when translated into English. The word *you* in English can refer to *you* as a big group, or just one of you. In the Greek, these pronouns mean *you* as a big group. In the South a better translation would be *ya'll*. The implication is clear. We need each other to live the Christian life. We need each other's prayers, encouragement, admonitions, and love. God never meant for us to live nearly as independently as most of us do. Mentoring is assumed in God's ideal church.

Eternal Community

The Bible reveals glorious truths about our eternal future in the book of Revelation, where Jesus gave John a related vision.

> After this I looked, and there before me was a great multitude that no one could count, from every nation, tribe, people and language, standing before the throne and before the Lamb. They were wearing white robes and were holding palm branches in their hands. And they cried out in a loud voice: "Salvation belongs to our God, who sits on the throne, and to the Lamb." (Rev. 7:9–10)

This passage, like many others that refer to our glorious future with Christ, contains *plural* pronouns. Not *I* and *me*, but *they* and *we*. We will experience these marvelous future events as a community of believers, so why not get intimately acquainted now? We can't live in a way that pleases God without one another.

SUMMARY

We observe community in the Trinity, the Garden, the nation Israel, and the church, and we see it prophesied in our future. Clearly God values community, and understanding this truth should motivate us to invest time, energy, and resources into building strong intergenerational communities. Healthy mentoring between the generations is better realized when the church becomes tightly knit like the redwood trees. Community is the place where mentors and mentees find one another and anchor deeply as they grow together. Intergenerational communities create places where organic matches occur naturally.

Some communities provide multiple opportunities to connect with other generations. Some don't. If you worship where community is weak, invest to strengthen it. If your community already provides these opportunities, rejoice and continue working to keep these connections strong.

Community is great. And then the people show up. When people show up, a group becomes the place where mess happens. But that mess may prove to be the answer to our prayers. It may become the catalyst for, the byproduct of and the environment in which discipleship happens. We move from being a program to the body of Christ, and we become the body of Christ broken and battered and bloodied and poured out for those around us. The body of Christ where community and redemption are found.

Heather Zempel[6]

6   Heather Zempel, *Community Is Messy* (Downers Grove, IL: InterVarsity Press, 2012), 45.

As a child and teenager I had many interactions with older people in my church because we all attended services together. In my college years, my church decided to have two worship services; traditional and contemporary. At that point, all the older people in church began going to the earlier traditional service and the young people went to the later contemporary service. I was saddened when I saw this happen because I knew that all the younger kids in the church would never have the chance to develop relationships with the older generation of churchgoers. Some of the relationships I formed with older women in my church I cherished deeply. I had so many examples of strong Christian women to look up to, and the younger girls didn't get that.

Holly, age 28

I grew up going to a house church on Wednesday nights that was intergenerational because the church was so small. I often look back and miss being in a group like that where everyone could learn from each other. The past ten years, my community groups have always been mid-age single adults or all females of the same age, and while we can all share the same season of life experiences, there's so much we're missing by not being with older and younger women. These opportunities to intermix do have to be created and, unfortunately, so many churches aren't creating them. I'm from the South but my experience was the same when I went up north for half a year. I was shocked to visit several churches where the entire church felt like it was all one age group, all single or newly married. As much as I enjoyed being with folks my age / season of life, I decided not to go back because I knew I wanted to be in a place with older people that I could learn from and that would help lead the body.

Ashley, age 35

At a church I went to in college I participated in a Bible Study / mentorship with the older women of the church. The girls would meet once a week with the women, and the older women would teach us a recipe, and while dinner was cooking we would all meet in a group, then break up into small groups to discuss the study. After the study we would sit around a big table and just talk about life and the study. It was such an easy and relaxed way to converse and get to know the older women of the church while also learning a practical skill (cooking) that I think most girls want to master. At the end of the study the women put together a cookbook for us with all the recipes we learned and us girls also submitted some of our favorite recipes to make.

Andrea, age 30

CHAPTER 8

The New Place of Technology: Your Digital Connections

I have much to write to you, but I do not want to use paper and ink. Instead, I hope to visit you and talk with you face to face, so that our joy may be complete.

2 John 12

In John's day, "pen and ink" was the communication tool he was tasked with evaluating, and though it might seem low tech to us today, it too had its detractors. A few hundred years before John wrote his letters, the Greek philosopher Socrates expressed concern about the technology of writing. He believed that learning in dialogue was the key to helping people grow in wisdom, and he worried that writing would make people knowledgeable, but it would fail to make them wise. Socrates was so worried about the damage that writing could cause that he never wrote any of his own ideas down.

John Dyer[1]

---

1   John Dyer, *From the Garden to the City: The Redeeming and Corrupting Power of Technology* (Grand Rapids: Kregel, 2011), 30.

Online, we easily find "company" but are exhausted by the pressures of performance. We enjoy continual connection but rarely have each other's full attention. We can have instant audiences but flatten out what we say to each other in new reductive genres of abbreviation. . . . we like being able to reach each other almost instantaneously but have to hide our phones to force ourselves to take a quiet moment.

Sherry Turkle[2]

A CARDINAL MENTORING RULE

Our chapel speaker had his young seminary audience on the edge of their seats—until he disparaged their use of technology. Just one critical quip about what felt normal and useful from their postmodern perspectives and this modern speaker suddenly morphed into a dinosaur right there on stage. For them his words and wisdom were now outdated and discarded. He might as well have concluded his message and sat down.

We mentors risk the same disconnect if we denigrate our charge's natural affinity for the latest technological devices. The rift between women who use technology and those who don't creates the digital divide. But does this mean that to mentor effectively in the twenty-first century we Moderns must become savvy techies? Yes and no.

No, in the sense that we will never do life online the way our children do, and they won't be as "at home" with technology as their children. If you are a Modern reading this, your experience is probably similar. I (Sue) remember playing a computer game with my four-year-old grandson. His fingers easily outworked mine, and when we needed instruction to move to another level, he instantly found aid on another site, but needed help to read the words. At least I could read better than he could! Yet even though when it comes to technology we are "immigrants" instead of "natives," we still need to understand the impact of technology and figure out how to use it.

---

2   Sherry Turkle, *Alone Together: Why We Expect More From Technology and Less From Each Other* (New York: Basic Books, 2011), 280.

Generational Uses of Technology

I use technology to access and share information. No more waiting hours or days for someone to get back to me. No more trips to the library to find articles or statistics. Efficiency levels have skyrocketed and I love it! My kids also use technology to access and share information, but in addition they use it regularly to stay connected with friends through social networking. I'm more likely to use technology to set up a face-to-face coffee with a friend. I'm still watching television for news and entertainment; my kids get theirs online when it fits their schedules. If I want details, I make a phone call. Not my kids. And as sure as I purchase what I think is the newest device, another takes its place—and my kids bought it last year. This whirlwind of new gadgets and the pressure to understand them makes my brain tired and leaves me feeling impaired and obsolete.

Thank goodness what we offer Postmoderns in a mentoring relationship is not our technological expertise. They can get that from a multitude of other sources. What we offer is harder to come by and something younger women crave: the wisdom to live well in a challenging world. That includes helping our mentees evaluate their own use of digital tools. But we won't be able to reach them if first we pooh-pooh their technology. They will immediately dismiss us as so out of touch that we couldn't possibly "get" them or their world. The cardinal rule as we interact with our mentees: DO NOT CRITICIZE THEIR TECHNOLOGY! It's here to stay and it hasn't taken God by surprise. In time, as your mentees grow in Christ, you will want to help them understand the positives and negatives of technology. But that's after they learn to trust you.

The Mentor's Attitude Toward Technology

As a mentor, your attitude toward technology will affect your mentoring relationships. Some of us embrace technological advances easily. We enjoy tackling how it works and what it will do for us. We use technology to reach children, grandchildren, or friends for our own benefit and to "keep up" with the times. Others of us find technology baffling and prefer to ignore it. But if we adopt "ain't it awful" attitudes, we will appear archaic to younger women. If we remain completely clueless, staying in touch with our mentees will probably be more difficult since technology is their natural means of contacting us, and the "click" talked about in Chapter 4 may be affected. Younger women won't believe that we have the capacity to understand their world if we cannot understand their technology. A recent study of Japanese children backs this up. Researchers found that children with cell phones seldom befriended children who did not own one.[3]

If you sense God leading you to become more proficient with technology, consider reverse mentoring. In Chapter 6 we suggested that younger women want to feel they can contribute to the mentoring relationship too. What if you asked a younger woman to teach you some basics? You will probably find she will delight in the opportunity, and you'll have fun exploring together.

EVALUATING TECHNOLOGY

Although we all have different comfort levels with technology, we are wise to evaluate how technology impacts our spiritual growth. Those who embrace technology without considering its negative effects usually stunt their spiritual progress without knowing it. Those who take an ostrich stance, denying that technology is changing the world, will experience frustration in their efforts to connect with most young women today. And those who bemoan that all technology is Satan's instrument to usher in chaos and disaster will send most young women heading for the exit as fast as they can run. None of these approaches is helpful in analyzing technology and its effects on our lives or on our mentoring relationships. We need to consider the positives and negatives, the possibilities and the dangers. We hope the following discussion equips you to manage technology in your own life and help your mentee use technology prudently.

Generational Thinking about Technology

John Dyer, author of *From the Garden to the City:, The Redeeming and Corrupting Power of Technology*, writes,

---

3   April Frawley Birdwell, "Addicted to Phones?" *The Post: Newsletter for the University of Florida Health Science Center:*, August 10, 2010, http://news.health.ufl.edu/media/2012/01/ThePost_Feb07.pdf.

When it comes to technology, each generation sees the issue from a slightly different perspective. Douglas Adams, author of *Hitchhiker's Guide to the Galaxy*, once grouped technology into three categories. First, "everything that's already in the world when you're born is just normal." Then, "anything that gets invented between then and before you turn thirty is incredibly exciting and creative and with any luck you can make a career out of it." Finally, "anything that gets invented after you're thirty is against the natural order of things and the beginning of the end of civilisation (sic) as we know it until it's been around for about ten years when it gradually turns out to be alright really."[4]

Every generation wrestles to adapt to new inventions. Gutenberg's printing press made books available to common people. Before his invention, priests and rabbis copied books by hand, making them rare and expensive. But we forget that the printed word, an invention we love and take for granted, had a serious downside. Before printed books, people relied on and developed their memory. Stories were passed from generation to generation, word for word, stored in highly developed human memory banks.

My (Sue) peer mentor and closest friend during the first decade of my Christian life was almost completely blind. Yet her memory was amazing! She remembered phone numbers, recipes, and Bible verses with incredible accuracy. She had to. Otherwise she would have been extremely limited, and she refused to accept any hindrance that might diminish her witness for Christ. She learned people's names, recognizing them by the shape of their profile and their voices. She taught the Bible to women without notes. She even snow skied and took scuba-diving lessons to meet nonbelievers. God used her blindness to woo many to faith. Had she lived before the printing press, her well-developed memory would have been normal, but today most of us rely on the written word and most of us struggle to even remember people's names. No doubt naysayers perceived Gutenberg's invention as a harbinger

---

4   John Dyer, *From the Garden to the City,* 26. Douglas Adams, comment on "How to Stop Worrying and Learn to Love the Internet," douglasadams.com blog, comment posted on September 1, 1999, http://www.douglasadams.com/dna/19990901-00-a.html.

of doom, and we hear similar warnings about ways technology is changing how people think, learn, and relate. Some are true; some are exaggerated.

Benefits of Technology

With each new technology comes change—benefits and losses, and each new generation learns to adapt. How can technology benefit God's work? Consider the global ramifications. A woman missionary can join a group of friends as they discuss a Bible passage they have studied. Put a mini-cam in the middle of the table and let her join in. Imagine the boost to women on the mission field who need support, encouragement, and prayer.

Technology connects us globally. Global Media Outreach (globalmediaoutreach.com) uses the Internet to help people find Jesus and disciple new believers. Online missionaries volunteer to build personal relationships with seekers and new believers all over the world. This nonprofit organization claims it reached 50 million people for Christ by May 2013.

Corrupt, abusive governments used to secretly exploit and mistreat their citizens and no one knew. But today a bystander films the abuse and puts the pictures online to expose the brutality. With twenty-four-hour news coverage, the whole world can express outrage immediately. More humane treatment and justice result, due to the quick communication that's now possible through technology.

Think about the possibilities for equipping Christian leaders all over the world. I (Sue) taped several sessions of one of my seminary courses to be used in China. The Asian professor who oversaw the project will show Chinese students my taped lectures. He will then teach the interactive parts of the course in their own language. He'll enjoy ongoing face-to-face encounters with these students as he teaches them what he knows about ministry in China, an area of the world where I'm clueless.

Ponder the benefit of staying connected with friends from the past. My (Sue) father was a lifer in the Coast Guard, and we were stationed for three years in Rhodes, Greece, when I was a teenager. After almost fifty years, a classmate friended me on Facebook and we enjoyed a reunion. What marvelous opportunities for fellowship and witnessing. While we lived on that Aegean island, we received a letter from my grandparents several times a year, but I did not hear their voices or see them the entire time. Today, through technology I can see and talk with my grandchildren who live in another state as often as I like.

My Bible study group leader, Elaine, works as a nurse for an insurance company—and it's all done from the comfort of her home. My husband worked for an international company and used to travel a lot—expensive, exhausting, and hard on the family. But today he and his coworkers can connect on conference calls, sometimes at 3 a.m. to accommodate the guy in India, but it saves time and money. Through technology, moms and dads are finding ways to work from home and be more involved in the lives of their children, a change that could strengthen future families and generations.

Benefits in Mentoring

My friend Pam mentors women of all generations: her students, her Bible study group, and her friends. Women are drawn to her caring demeanor and servant's heart. She's in her sixties and finds technology challenging, but she's persevered to understand and use some of it in order to stay connected with younger women. Her persistence paid off with Megan.

Megan lived in the townhouse across from Pam, and for several years, like many neighbors today, their relationship consisted of a friendly wave when passing or a momentary encounter at the mailbox. But when Megan's life began to unravel, a mutual friend encouraged her to ask Pam for guidance.

One morning before work, Megan knocked on Pam's door and asked if they could meet. Pam replied, "Sure, just text me and we'll set up a time." Megan responded, "WOW! You text. My mother won't text. That would be great!" They exchanged numbers and the next week set up a meeting through text messaging. Megan's life was full and she had no interest in setting up a weekly connection. Instead she wanted to meet when the need arose. So for the next couple of years she and Pam would meet, prompted by a text to set up a mutually convenient time.

Pam would have preferred regular get-togethers, the way she was mentored when she was Megan's age, and she would have preferred to set up their times together on the phone or by email. To Pam, a weekly time together felt more like real mentoring, and Pam described their relationship as a little like "crisis management." But their off-and-on relationship fit Megan's needs perfectly and added value to her life.

Pam accommodated Megan by using Megan's preferred communication style, and over time, the hours they spent together helped Megan immeasurably. Their relationship qualified as precious and profitable mentoring from Megan's perspective. Pam's willingness to learn and use texting spoke volumes to Megan about Pam's acceptance of her world. Pam's attitude paved the way to a heart connection that enriched both their lives.

Screen-to-Screen vs. Face-to-Face

Technology also allowed Pam and Megan to stay connected after Megan moved to another city. In a mobile world, technology helps us continue mentoring relationships after one of us relocates. Not ideal but still profitable. We believe that face-to-face mentoring friendships work best, but once the face-to-face connection is strong, mentoring can continue through technology.

Face-to-face is better because it facilitates knowing and loving each other with an otherwise impossible depth, although not all Postmoderns would agree. More and more young people are settling for a short digital shout out instead of a phone call or personal conversation. The shout out is quick, fits their schedule, doesn't involve small talk, and is almost never messy. In 2012, North Americans ages eighteen to twenty-nine sent and received an average of eighty-eight texts per day.[5]

Eighty-eight texts a day! But what is the quality of that connection? Is there time left for reflection on conversations, information, or experiences? How much alone time is left? A day composed of so many texts is full of relational connections—yet young people tell us they have fewer *real* friends today than in the past. Their moments are crowded with digital shout outs and yet, as Sherry Turkle, MIT techno-guru, puts it, young folk are "alone together."[6] In all the flurry and fuss, many are aching, yearning for authentic connection. Thus their quest for a mentor who looks them in the eye, listens intently, and shares from the heart. Yet, don't be surprised if your mentee, despite her yearning, may be relationally immature. This won't be true of all young women, so be careful not to stereotype. Some young women exhibit excellent

---

5   Jeffrey Kluger, "We never talk any more: The problem with text messaging," from TIME Mobility Poll, CNN, http://cnn.com/2012/08/31/tech/mobile/problem-text-messaging-oms.

6   Sherry Turkle, *Alone Together*. This quote is taken from the book title.

relational skills, but the more young women withdraw behind abbreviated texts and screens, the more likely their interpersonal competence will suffer. Understand that some young women who need your love, attention, and guidance may not possess the relational skills that you possessed at their age. You may wrongly assume that these skills are natural for everyone. They wouldn't be natural for you either if much of your communication consisted of abbreviated shortcuts rather than eye-to-eye connections. Part of your stealth curriculum may be to gently and patiently teach your mentee the beauty, richness, and wonder of face-to-face exchange. Conversations that connect people deeply require practice. Relational skills are learned over time, through trial and error, stepping out and messing up. The beauty of humanness is the ability to communicate at soul level, to read each other's tone of voice and inflections, to interpret facial expressions and touch. These skills are developed as we grow in our capacity to love, empathize, share, grieve, and join together in these made-in-the-image-of-God human moments.

But for some, soul connections are scary. They require vulnerability, with the potential for hurt and misunderstanding. Moving away from face-to-face connections can be signs of protective postures.

Habitual texters may not only cheat their existing relationships, they can also limit their ability to form future ones since they don't get to practice the art of interpreting nonverbal visual cues. There's a reason it's so easy to lie to small kids ("Santa really, truly did bring those presents") and that's because they're functional illiterates when it comes to reading inflection and facial expressions. As with real reading, the ability to comprehend subtlety and complexity comes only with time and a lot of experience. If you don't adequately acquire those skills, moving into the real world of real people can actually become quite scary. "I talk to kids and they describe their fear of conversation," says Turkle. "An 18-year-old I interviewed recently said, 'Someday, but certainly not now, I want to learn to have a conversation.'"[7]

---

7   Kluger, *We never talk any more,* http://cnn.com/2012/08/31/tech/mobile/prob-lem-text-messaging-oms)

Yet within each of us remains a deep desire to love and be loved, to know and be known, to understand and be understood. Thus the tension for the avid or addicted digitizer. When a mentee seeks out a mentor, she may be calling for help, a first step in climbing out of a deep pit where she is safe but alone. A three-dimensional encounter through physical presence involves an unexplainable something that can't be matched on a screen or through a device.

Tim Challies, pastor and author of *The Next Story: Life and Faith After the Digital Explosion,* reminds us that no young man says to his girlfriend, "I just can't wait to write you a letter." Instead he says, "I just can't wait to see you."[8] During my senior year in high school, I (Sue) developed a relationship with a pen pal, a girl my age from Mexico City. We wrote letters back and forth, beautiful letters, in preparation for the time she spent at my home and the time I spent at hers as exchange students. When I think of Rocio, I remember our face-to-face adventures exploring one another's worlds in person. Letters filled in gaps between visits, but the richest experiences consisted of weeks of physical presence.

As believers, we look forward to God's promise that we will see Him face-to-face:

> When I was a child, I talked like a child, I thought like a child, I reasoned like a child. When I became a man, I put the ways of childhood behind me. For now we see only a reflection as in a mirror; then we shall see face to face. Now I know in part; then I shall know fully, even as I am fully known. (1 Cor. 13:11–12)

Our souls instinctively long for the intimacy that only personal contact provides. But when face to face isn't possible, a digital connection can be the next best thing. Once depth is established, conversing through digital means can reinforce our relationships.

Charlotte graduated from our seminary and moved to South Africa where she ministered to children. Before she moved, I (Sue) enjoyed a

---

8   Tim Challies, "iDolatry: Christian Blogger/Pastor Warns of Misplaced Affections," *Trak*, October, 2011,12, 13.

friendship with her that took on a mentoring flavor. Later on the mission field, she needed a course in teaching the Bible to women, so I tweaked my face-to-face course to accommodate her. We interacted on Skype, and she taped her messages to African women for my evaluation. Our earlier face-to-face friendship made the secondary connection work much better than it would have if I had never known her.

As we move further away from the Modern era and further into the Postmodern digital age, we'll experience more and more unheard of benefits to enrich the lives of people everywhere; however, losses also accompany the dramatic changes we're experiencing due to the whole-hearted without-assessment embrace of technology. Wise mentors identify the negative side effects and graciously alert mentees to the down sides of excessive or naive use of technology. We hope the following section helps you.

LOSSES

Whenever drastic change occurs in a society, as everyone adjusts, leaders must carefully assess unforeseen damages. Unfortunately technological advances sweep down on us like an avalanche, with such speed and fury that we have little time to evaluate their impact before another comes along just as powerfully behind it. Advertisers and talk shows hail these inventions as new and glorious steps toward progress, and indeed many are. Eager shoppers wait in line, sometimes all night, to be first to purchase the next gadget or its upgrade. These advances will continue to roll out and change culture, communication, and lifestyles.

But just as Gutenberg's printing press impacted human memory, we will experience losses in the postmodern era too. They will affect our mentees and our mentoring relationships and will saddle us, the mentors, with the responsibility to lovingly help our mentees overcome unhealthy attitudes and actions toward technology. How can we gently woo them to use technology in ways that foster their spiritual growth, their love of God, and their overall spiritual health? That's our task. But first we must understand some of the specific losses that accompany unexamined habits.

Shallow Thinking, Short Attention Spans and Inability to Focus

If your mentee spends hours every day surfing the web and hopscotching between sites, her ability to focus and think deeply may be effected. Nicholas Carr writes:

> Dozens of studies by psychologists, neurobiologists, educators, and Web designers point to the same conclusion: when we go online, we enter an environment that promotes cursory reading, hurried and distracted thinking, and superficial learning. It's possible to think deeply while surfing the Net, just as it's possible to think shallowly while reading a book, but that's not the type of thinking the technology encourages and rewards.[9]

I'm (Sue) finding that more and more young students struggle to read a whole book or think deeply. Many of my millennial students are convinced that they can listen to me teach, look at sites related to what I'm saying, check their email, shop, even watch videos (if the sound doesn't give them away and distract others), and still do well on my tests. But studies refute that assumption.

Two researchers at Cornell divided students into two groups. While the professor taught, the first group was allowed to do whatever they liked online. The second group heard the same professor teach the same material, but the students were not allowed to use technology. Then both groups were tested to see how much they learned. The students surfing the Net performed significantly more poorly than those who were not distracted by other media.[10] What are some of the dangers of all this dipping in and out of screens? Tim Challies sites two examples:

> All of this distraction is reshaping us in two dangerous ways. First we are tempted to forsake quality for quantity, believing

---

9 Nicholas Carr, *The Shallows: What the Internet Is Doing to Our Brains* (New York: Norton, 2011), 115–116.
10 Ibid., 130–131.

the lie that virtue comes through speed, productivity, and efficiency. . . . And second . . . we lose our ability to engage in deeper ways of thinking—concentrated, focused thought that requires time and cannot be rushed. Instead of focusing our efforts in a *few* directions, we give scant attention to many things, skimming instead of studying. We live rushed lives and forget how to move slowly, carefully, and thoughtfully through life. . . . We need to relearn how to think, and we need to discipline ourselves to think deeply, conquering the distractions in our lives so that we can *live* deeply. We must rediscover how to be truly thoughtful Christians, as we seek to live with virtue in the aftermath of the digital explosion.[11]

I (Barbara) was astounded when a twenty-six-year-old youth leader told me about her "technology box." She meets weekly with a group of high school girls for Bible study. Frustration with their short attention spans pushed her over the edge; not one of them could go more than two or three minutes without sending, receiving, or checking for a text message. The continual distraction made quality discussion impossible, so she decorated a box and set it by the door. She now requires each girl to drop all her technology in the box when she enters the room and retrieve it when Bible study is over. By their reaction, you would think the leader had taken away their food for three days. We know the problem is serious when a digitally connected twenty-six-year-old has had it.

Thank goodness shallow thinking, short attention spans, and inability to focus are not permanent. Research tells us that our brains are malleable. They change shape and function according to how we use them. The good news is that reduced capacities can be redeemed. Ironically, Nicolas Carr, author of *The Shallows: What the Internet Is Doing to Our Brains,* found his own concentration effected by technology as he attempted to write his book. As a result, he left a highly wired life in Boston for the mountains of Colorado where he digitized down. He says the experience was far from painless, but

---

11   Tim Challies, *The Next Story: Life and Faith After the Digital Explosion* (Grand Rapids: Zondervan, 2011), 117.

in time he was able to sit at his keyboard for hours at a time, focused and deeply immersed in the work. He writes, "I started to feel generally calmer and more in control of my thoughts—less like a lab rat pressing a lever and more like, well, a human being. My brain could breathe again."[12]

We're not advocating that you encourage your mentees to relocate to the mountains, but we're suggesting that some of them may need to develop a sensitivity to poor or excessive use of technology. All of us should be asking ourselves, "Is my thinking more shallow than in the past? Is my attention span reduced? Am I struggling with an increased inability to focus?" If the answer is *yes* to any of these questions, a hard look at our digital lives is in order. We applaud Carr for writing, "We shouldn't allow the glories of technology to blind our inner watchdog to the possibility that we've numbed an essential part of our self."[13]

New Spiritual Disciplines to Counter an Over-digitized Life

In time, we may need to help our mentees develop spiritual disciplines to curb excessive or unwise use of technology. These excesses are not limited to any generation, so first you, as mentor, may need to practice these spiritual disciplines yourself. Then, after your mentee trusts you and you sense the timing is appropriate, brainstorm together how you both can use technology more wisely. Below are a few suggestions:

Before Adding Another Digital Device, Ask Questions. Make questions part of your technological purchases. In addition to checking out design, digital capability, and charge life, ask questions like

- Will it *really* make me more productive? In my vocational life? In my personal life?
- What is my motivation for including this device in my life?
- Is this device a good use of my financial resources?
- Will it help me become a fully developed Christ follower?

---

12 Nicolas Carr, *The Shallows*, 190.
13 Ibid., 212.

- Will this device simplify my life or complicate it?
- Will this device encourage or discourage closer family ties? community ties?
- Will this device feed addictive or unhealthy behavior patterns in my life?
- If I add this device, should I eliminate another?

How about bouncing answers off one another? Discussing these kinds of questions will facilitate deep thinking as to why we do what we do and help us become more astute stewards of our resources, as well as more skilled at in-depth communication.

Implement Periodic Digital Fasts. Fasting involves turning away from our habitual routines and toward more focused times with God, not to manipulate God to do our will, but to spend extended time with Him, to know Him better and discern *His* will.

When I (Sue) was a seminary student, a professor explained why we typically link fasting with food. Throughout history, women spent most of their day preparing meals. They walked to the market to secure food for that day's menu, baked bread from scratch, and killed, dressed, and cooked meat when it was available. He insisted that fasting from meals was God's way of giving women a break from routine tasks and encouraging them to spend quality time with God. In our digital world of microwave ovens and prepackaged foods, today many women spend more time online than preparing food or on other menial tasks. Digital fasts are probably more helpful than food fasts for women more tethered to their tablets than to their kitchens.

We envision women gathering to examine their online lives at new retreat centers, farms, or ranches designed to remove women from digital environments by blocking all Internet access and digital connections. Women would learn about and practice new kinds of spiritual disciplines to help them overcome digital addictions or unhealthy tendencies, possibly in the form of digital detox seminars. For example, a workshop might teach women to engage in lengthy, deep, and meaningful conversations with others. Instead of zip lines and competitive games, these retreat centers could teach participants to read lengthy articles *slowly* and then discuss what they learned, guided by licensed digital detox counselors. These experts would help women lengthen their attention spans, think deep thoughts, and sharpen their focus. They would teach women how to use technology without succumbing to dangerous excesses or "tech-brain syndrome."

You may think we are exaggerating the dangers, but in China, Taiwan, and Korea, the DSM (handbook for psychologists and psychiatrists)[14] already lists Internet Addiction Disorder (IAD), calling it problematic Web use and a grave national health crisis. The United States is close behind. As Christian mentors we are responsible to help our protégés wean themselves off what is fast becoming the drug of choice for too many Christians. If we don't exercise restraint, technology can woo any of us away from a deep, intimate relationship with God and each other.

Seek wisdom. The book of Proverbs exhorts us to search for wisdom as one of the most prized possessions in life. We are wise when we understand the way the world works and know what to do as each situation presents itself. Wisdom is skill in living. It's one of the end goals of the Christian life, but poor use of technology can hinder our acquisition of wisdom.

Our minds function like a computer, with part of it divided into categories or folders (sorry for the unfortunate analogy). As you grow up, you learn more and more about how life works. For example, let's say that in kindergarten you learn that God loves you. You may or may not understand what love really means, depending on your experience with love in your family, but you begin the process of discovering what love is.

As you journey on to elementary school, you learn more about love. You hear different definitions of love, and you tuck them away in that "love" folder in your mind. Every time you sit through a lesson or have an experience related to love, you add to the folder. As you mature, your understanding of the concept of love deepens, and you develop capacities to distinguish between different kinds of love. If you are exposed to Scripture, your understanding of God's love becomes more and more acute. If you are wounded by love, you understand that love can hurt. If you experience God's love in your life, you add that understanding to the folder, and so on.

---

14 American Psychiatric Association, *Diagnostic and Statistical Manual of Mental Disorders, 5th Edition: DSM-5* (American Psychiatric Association: Arlington, VA, 2013).

Ultimately if you continue to think deep thoughts about love, you become wise about love—what it is, the difference between God's love and people's love, how to give it and receive it, and how to discern real love from a shabby counterfeit. But this only occurs if you reflect on your experiences, interact with others, think deeply, and allow these insights to move from your head to your heart and finally out in the way you treat others. What happens if you shut down the process because it's hard or painful or time consuming? You never become the fully human person you were created to be. In healthy mentoring, mentor and mentee help one another move forward in their desire to become wise women, with the mentor guiding because she has a head start.

SUMMARY

In this chapter we've talked about the reality that we have entered into a digital age, with its benefits and losses. Technology is changing certain aspects of mentoring relationships, and it's changing all of us with each passing year. Technology affects the way we learn, think, and relate to others. It's shaping our relationship with Christ. Again, we speak in broad swaths, since every individual and relationship is different. But your mentees *are* influenced by technology, and knowing how will help you love and guide them into the new world that awaits them.

I can't stress enough how important technology is in the mentoring relationship with a Millennial. Finding a mentor that's on Facebook is pretty essential. I'd like to be able to see the life my mentor lives, and Facebook is a great way to "stalk" that person. It's great if the mentor texts which practically everyone does now, I think, LOL. My life is all digital and there's no way I have the time or interest to sit down and hand-write lessons or studies. It's encouraging to have a mentor who at least has an online presence and can offer encouragement by sending articles, notes, etc. I don't think there's any way I could sustain my end of a mentoring relationship without my mentor having Facebook, email, texting, etc.

Sharon, age 32

I'm not a huge techy. I use social networking only minimally… but I do love to text. The thing that I find great about it is that I can send thoughts to friends and family that would otherwise be lost completely—just little tidbits that happen throughout the day that I would probably never remember to bring up when we were able to meet face to face. My closest friend and I text a lot; neither of us like to talk on the phone and both have small kids who prevent conversation even if we liked the phone! But we've also realized that texting just doesn't cut it in terms of maintaining a true friendship. We actually schedule times to meet a month in advance, just to make sure we get the face-to-face time. We see each other more than this usually, but not always with the hectic pace of life! My husband and I also text a lot when he travels for work. It allows us to keep in contact without having to try to carve out time for a conversation, most of which consists of factual information, after the kids are in bed and we are both exhausted from our days. So texting can be a great supplement, but yes, women need to be pushed toward actual in-person conversation if they aren't doing this.

If you will embrace texting, though, you might really enjoy the interactions you are able to have with younger women using this medium! It's often all about sharing lighthearted stories, pictures, and encouraging thoughts with people you don't get to see as often as you'd like. You'd be amazed how much you can lift a younger woman's spirit just by sending a text every once in a while that says "I was thinking about you today! How was the meeting?" or something of that nature.

I am pretty much completely dependent on technology for organization of my schedule, though. Keeping my calendar straight and communicating about events, including something like meeting with a mentor, pretty much won't happen if it isn't on my phone. Even email and Facebook are really not accessible enough when it comes to scheduling my world.

Joy, age 36

EPILOGUE

For the Joy...

I have just come from a gathering of women. For three hours this morning, the four of us sat in a local restaurant, sharing our needs, our concerns, our unanswered questions—our hearts. Two of us cried after deep confessionals; we all laughed. . . When it was time to go—as other commitments called—we ran outside into the spring rain, lighthearted as children out for recess. . . [1]

Brenda Hunter captures the exhilarating joy possible through mentoring connections, whether in groups or one-on-one. We've experienced that joy, and we want you to experience it too. Dynamic mentoring relationships are one of God's priceless treasures, not only in our lives but in the lives of younger women we touch. Blessings of healthy mentoring relationships include:

- Women connect out of mutual trust and love.
- They understand one another and love each other anyway.
- One is farther down the road in her journey, and when appropriate, she gives the other direction in light of her failures and successes, but she doesn't expect the other to mimic her journey.
- Each, regardless of age, believes that she can learn from the other.
- Each can be herself, nothing to lose, nothing to prove.

---

1   Brenda Hunter, *In the Company of Women* (Sisters, OR: Multnomah, 1994), 17.

- Each listens and values the other's ideas even if she doesn't always agree.
- Even if one says something stupid, the other will view it through the lens of love and give her the benefit of the doubt.
- But each also cares enough to gently step in and help the other back on course if one of them is on the verge of doing something dangerous.
- The basis of the relationship is love for the Lord, and each points the other to Him.

But these sweet gifts could soon qualify for the endangered list. We are experiencing a mentoring crisis. Generational differences threaten the future of mentoring. We Moderns stand with one foot in the modern era and another in the postmodern era. An ever-widening gap makes the stance uncomfortable, tenuous, and unstable. Unless we seek God's guidance, confront generational misunderstandings, and seize opportunities to use what we learn, young women will drown in a hostile sea of cultural relativism, chaos, and hopelessness.

Lost at Sea

Our beloved mentor at Dallas Theological Seminary, Howard Hendricks, told a story that pictures our challenge. He wrote,

> Drowning victims often fight their rescuers in the hysteria of that terrifying moment. The same is often true for those who are floundering spiritually because their faith has suffered shipwreck.
>
> A young man who strayed from the Lord was finally brought back by the help of a friend who really loved him. When there was full repentance and restoration, I asked this Christian how it felt while he was away from God. The young man said it seemed like he was out to sea, in deep water, in deep trouble, and all his friends were on the shoreline hurling accusations at him about justice, penalty, and wrong.

"But there was one Christian brother who actually swam out to get me and would not let me go. I fought him, but he pushed aside my fighting, grasped me, put a life jacket around me, and took me to shore. By the grace of God, he was the reason I was restored. He would not let me go."[2]

Rescued by Love

Too many young women feel like they are drowning, and in their terror may look like they are putting up a fight, but down deep they really do want to know how to develop a real relationship with God. They want to know how life works, and they are wide open to learning from an older woman who loves, understands, and respects them. To rescue them, we must swim out to where they are, wrap life jackets around them, and bring them back to shore. We'll need strength, sound judgment, and perseverance. We must be willing to deep-six heavy weights that frustrate our rescue efforts, like generational preferences and outdated styles and practices that some of us cling to for dear life. But if we don't rid ourselves of these anchors, we will lose these precious young women to dangerous worldly undercurrents.

Jesus rescued us with love, and He calls us to extend the arms of life to the next generation. After He sacrificed His life so we might live, He experienced the joy of resurrection. Whose desperate cries are calling to you over the roaring waves? And what joys await you if you're brave enough to trust God and dive in after them?

---

2   Howard G. Hendricks, quoted in *The Tale of the Tardy Oxcart: And 1501 Other Stories,* Charles R. Swindoll (Nashville: Word, 1998), 487.

APPENDIX A

Mentor's Training Tools and Tips

We designed this manual to help leaders train others to be effective mentors in light of the massive changes we have highlighted. Use all or parts of this material in small groups, classes, seminars, or weekly training sessions.

We have divided the training into six sessions and a final gathering to celebrate with potential mentees. You may want to combine parts, or skip some, depending on your time frame and the needs of the participants. You might present this material in a one or two-day workshop, or you might spread the material out over a number of weeks. You can use all of it or pick and choose the parts that work best for you. If your time is limited a *Fast Track* option for condensed training is available at the end of each training session.

Through different approaches and activities, we have attempted to reach every learner, helping different women process the material in different ways. Our goal is to help you encourage and equip older women to rise up as passionate insightful mentors in the twenty-first century.

However you decide to structure the training, we recommend that you encourage women to complete the training *before* they begin new mentoring relationships. First impressions are hard to change, and if you blow the initial contact, young women aren't likely to give it another try. Mentors who must let go of cherished methods need to first understand why. It may take time to develop new mentoring mind-sets, so be patient.

Training Session One

A New Problem: Outdated Methods

Training Goal

The purpose of this session is to awaken mentors to the reality that Christians face a serious problem related to mentoring in the twenty-first century. Due to massive cultural changes, mentoring styles and practices that worked in the past don't work today. By reading Chapter 1, taking the "Mentor's Self-Assessment," hearing from young women on a postmodern panel, and discussing their discoveries together, mentors should begin to process this information and what it means for them as a mentor. When they do, most future mentors will be ready and eager to learn more about generational differences, the topics highlighted in Sessions 2 and 3.

Participant's Home Assignment

Ask participants to complete the following assignments at home before the first training session:

- Take the "Mentor's Self Assessment" on page 197 and bring it to the session.
- Read the Prologue and Chapter 1 of *Organic Mentoring*.

You can find the book at amazon.com or your local book retailer.

Training Session

Assessment Discussion

Begin the training with a review of the "Mentor's Self-Assessment." Take a few minutes to discover where most of the mentors fall on the assessment. Were there any surprises?

Mentor's Self-Assessment Score
85–70   Strong preference for methods favored by the older generation

69–50 Moderately strong preference for methods favored by the older generation

49–35 Preferences characteristic of both generations

34–17 Preferences similar to the younger generation

Group Discussion

1. What were your impressions when you read Sharon's story?

2. Were you surprised when you read Ashley's impression of the mentoring experience? If so, why?

3. Why do you think current research reveals that as many as eight out of ten young women express dissatisfaction with their mentoring experiences?

4. Can you recall a specific time when you felt disconnected from younger generations? What happened and how did you feel?

5. What are your thoughts as you read the list of the differences in generational tendencies listed under "Where Do We Start?" on page 26?

6. What are we risking if older Christian women fail to effectively mentor younger Christian women?

7. How do you feel as you embark on learning how to mentor younger women today? Overwhelmed? Hopeless? Irritated? Discouraged? Excited?

Activity

A Postmodern Panel

Recruit three or four young women to participate on a postmodern panel. Select diverse young women you think will represent their generation well. Send the questions below to panel members to think about before they arrive, but don't be concerned if you don't use all the prepared-ahead questions. During the panel time, use them to "prime the pump."

Select a moderator to ask initial questions, keep time, and be sure the conversation moves along. A worthy goal is natural conversation that flows out of questions from the mentors to the panel members. Use the prepared questions in case of a lull.

Create the kind of atmosphere where the young women feel free to be honest in their answers. Don't allow the older women to shut down or judge the opinions of the younger women. Help the older women realize that the purpose of hearing the panel is to understand the perspectives of postmodern women, not to change the younger women's views.

After the panel members leave, debrief with the mentors. We have provided some questions to ask the older women as they consider what they heard.

Arranging for this kind of panel takes extra time and work, and you may think it's not worth the effort; however, we find that when older women hear from real women in their midst, they are more likely to be convinced of the need for change.

Panel Questions
1. Introduce yourself to the group. Briefly tell us about the important people in your life, how you spend a typical day.

2. How is your generation different from your parents' generation?

3. What qualities do you admire in older women? What would you look for in a mentor?

4. If you were mentored by an older woman, what would make it work well? What would hurt the relationship?

5. If you could say something helpful to older women who want to be effective mentors to women your age, what would you tell them?

Debriefing Questions *(after the panel guests leave)*
1. What was similar about the women on the panel? What was different?

2. What surprised you?

3. What did you learn that will help you be a more effective mentor to younger women?

4. What do you think will be your greatest asset in mentoring younger women today?

5. What do you think will be your greatest hindrance in mentoring younger women today?

Final Thoughts

When some women awaken to the truth that generational differences require change, they may experience anxiety, irritation, or even defensiveness. These older women may believe that when younger women "grow up," they will adopt the perspectives of the older generations. They may resist the idea that new mentoring styles and methods are needed.

If this occurs, let these women express their feelings without judgment, and don't try to change them. Pray and expect the Holy Spirit to work in the minds and hearts of the mentors during the training sessions. Let the women wrestle with these ideas, and together work through what they believe God wants to teach them. This is just the first session, and change for some is difficult. Trust God and move forward.

Fast Track

1. Before the training session, ask the mentors to take the "Mentor's Self-Assessment" and read the Prologue and Chapter 1 of *Organic Mentoring*. Remind them to take the assessment before reading the book.

2. During the training session, discuss questions 2, 5, and 6 under **Group Discussion.**

Training Session Two

A NEW GENERATION: UNDERSTANDING POSTMODERN WOMEN

Training Goal

The purpose of this training session is to expose older women to the values and challenges of potential mentees. These differences are real and have important implications for effective mentoring. For now, focus on the characteristics and struggles of a typical "younger woman" but emphasize the uniqueness of each individual. No stereotyping!

Participant's Home Assignment

Ask mentors to read Chapter 2 and jot down their impressions to aid in the group discussion.

TRAINING SESSION

Teaching Time

If you enjoy teaching, or know someone who does, one of you might prepare a brief teaching time where you present an abbreviated version of each postmodern value and challenge, as described in the chapter. After your summary explanation, you could list them on a board or in PowerPoint and ask if the women can add personal illustrations. You could follow this teaching vignette with small or large group discussion. Pray and ask God to help you create a teaching/discovery experience that will drive home the main points while giving women the opportunity to talk about their ideas and potential roadblocks.

Group Discussion

1. How do you think you would have reacted if you had been Carolyn, attempting to throw a shower with these millennial women?

2. What differences did you observe between the ways Carolyn and the younger women approached the task?

3. What problems can you foresee if Carolyn became a mentor to one or more of these young women?

4. As you read about "Postmodern Values," did you experience any "Aha" moments? If so, elaborate.

5. Review the "Challenges" listed on pages 44–49. Which have you observed in young women you know? (No names, please.)

6. Have any of your ideas about younger women changed as a result of reading more about generational tendencies? If so, please discuss.

Final Thoughts

Again, be sure you emphasize that when we study generational characteristics, we must be careful not to assume that everyone will reflect the same attributes. Stereotyping is dangerous because it places expectations on people, assuming they should all look or act a particular way. We study generational generalities to make us aware of tendencies, but we realize that there are many differences within these categories. When you talk about these characteristics, continually use language like "many," "tend to," "may appear." Stay away from absolutes in your language, or you will unwittingly teach stereotyping.

Are these future mentors beginning to warm up to the idea that these generational differences require new mentoring methods? Don't lose patience with those who resist. Change comes hard for some. Again, let them verbalize their ideas. Keep them thinking.

Fast Track

Note to Leader: We believe this training session is the most important. Understanding the next generation is foundational to successful mentoring in the twenty-first century. We recommend you do the full session. But, if you absolutely can't, use the Fast Track option.

1. Ask mentors to read Chapter 2 before the training session.

2. During the session briefly review the values and challenges of the postmodern generation.

3. Discuss questions 2, 4, and 5 under **Group Discussion**

Training Session Three

A NEW CHALLENGE: UNDERSTANDING OURSELVES

Training Goal

This session is designed to help mentors understand their own tendencies, values, and challenges because they affect their mentoring styles and practices. Explore why they exhibit some of these tendencies, and why mentoring younger generations may feel strange in light of who they are and what they value. Make sure they grasp and use terms like *modern* and *postmodern* correctly, because these terms will be used throughout the training and you want to make sure everyone is on the same page.

Participant's Home Assignment

Ask mentors to read Chapter 3 and jot down their impressions. In what ways do these generalities picture their tendencies? In what ways are they different?

TRAINING SESSION

Assessment Discussion

At the beginning of your session, have the mentors take "The Mentor's Perspective Assessment" on page 199. Discuss their findings. What did they learn about themselves?

Teaching Time

If you prepared and taught a lesson on the values and challenges of Postmoderns in the previous session, you may want to teach a similar lesson, outlining and contrasting the values and challenges of Moderns. You could create a learning experience to be sure they "get" the differences in these two era labels. You might divide the women into groups and ask them to come up with definitions for the terms *modern* and *postmodern*. Then compare and discuss their definitions and related ideas. You might conclude with asking these future mentors whether or not they relate to the different tendencies of their generation. Some will and some won't.

Again, you could follow this teaching vignette with small or large group discussion. Pray and ask God to help create a teaching/discovery experience that will drive home the main points you want them to remember while giving women the opportunity to talk about their ideas. If they exhibit differing opinions, help the women see them as opportunities to learn about one another rather than something to fear or correct. Point out that these interchanges, if respectful and polite, offer opportunities to practice listening to women with different opinions. Good practice for when they mentor younger women!

Group Discussion

1. As you read through the list of modern values, which ones did you identify with? Which ones did not describe you?

2. Even if you can't identify with all the modern values, did they reflect truths about your generation? If so, elaborate.

3. Are you a person who adapts quickly to change, or do you generally resist it? Give examples.

4. If you have made successful changes in your life, what helped you?

5. What are your thoughts as you compare values and challenges of younger women with the values and challenges of older women?

6. Who should be more adaptive to the other generation: older women or younger women? Who do you think is more capable of adapting and why?

Activities

Generations Collage

Divide the mentors into groups, and give each group a large poster board. Provide them with different kinds of magazines, online articles, and colored paper, as well as markers, scissors, glue, etc., and ask each group to design two collages. One side of the poster board should represent Moderns and the other side should represent Postmoderns. After they have completed the project, have teams explain their collages to the other teams. Think about giving prizes for different categories: for example, most attractive, most creative, most effective, most outside-the-box.

Possible Debriefing Questions for Collage

1. As you looked through media for your collages, what did you learn?

2. What additional insight did you glean from comparing the modern and postmodern generations during this exercise?

3. What is God teaching you as you work through this training about effective mentoring today?

Intergenerational Game
   Games teach. If your group enjoys games, order a book like *"52 Activities for Improving Cross-Cultural Communication"*[1] and try out some of the suggested activities. For example, on page eleven you'll find instructions for the *Alpha-Beta Partnership* game. I (Sue) successfully used this game to help women increase their sensitivity to women with different values and practices. Although this game requires significant preparation time, it's worth the investment. Set aside at least an hour to play the game, including time to debrief.

Final Thoughts

During this third session we hope you are beginning to see mentors coming to a new and deep understanding of the importance of grasping generational differences and why mentoring styles and practices must change. These first three sessions are foundational to the heart change that will be needed as mentors read and digest Part Two of *Organic Mentoring*.
   In the next training session, we'll look at specific new approaches to mentoring today. We'll explain how to make adjustments to build bridges

---

1   Donna M. Stringer and Patricia A. Cassiday, *52 Activities for Improving Cross-Cultural Communication* (Boston, MA: Intercultural Press, 2009).

to younger women, while still maintaining the essence and heart of mentoring. Pray fervently for the women in the training program as they move forward to develop dynamic mentoring skills for the twenty-first century.

Fast Track

1. Ask mentors to read Chapter 3 before the training session.

2. During the session briefly review the values and challenges of the older generation.

3. Discuss questions 2, 5, and 6 under **Group Discussion**.

Training Session Four

A New Focus: Initiating a Match That Works

Training Goal

The purpose of this session is to help mentors understand how to create effective mentoring relationships today. Mentors learn to release much of the process and place more responsibility in the hands of younger women. The following are important concepts to grasp:

- Why artificial matching doesn't work
- The importance of the compulsory click, as well as trust and attraction
- Why younger women must drive the selection process
- Why the focus must shift from mentor to mentee
- How these changes can benefit not only the mentee but also the mentor

Participant's Home Assignment

Ask mentors to read the introduction to Part Two and Chapter 4 and jot down notes that will aid in discussing what they learned.

Training Session

Activity

Skit

Kick off this training session with a skit. Ask several outgoing women who enjoy writing skits to create and perform two scenarios. Ask the skit writers to include as many concepts from the chapter as they can.

The first scenario (similar to Maribeth's experience in the chapter) should represent the initial relationship between two women who did not connect because of generational misunderstandings and the lack of the compulsory click. Feel free to make it funny.

The second scenario should represent the initial relationship between two women who do click, a relationship that shows promise of life change for both. Create several questions related to the skit to give to viewers. Write them on a handout. Challenge the viewers to think about these questions during the skit. Give them a few minutes to write down their answers, observations, and ideas after the skit.

Skit Debrief and Discussion
A facilitator leads a discussion about the skit. What did you learn? Why did the first initial connection fail while the second one worked?

Teaching Time

Ask a woman who enjoys teaching to pull out core concepts from the main sections of Chapter 4. She might write them on a board, or present a PowerPoint, give some examples, or ask the participants to discuss the concepts. Can they add personal experiences? What might be challenging for them? Do they sense any roadblocks that make this approach difficult?

Group Discussion

1. What do you think about a mentoring approach that feels less organized, predictable, and measurable? Why do you think older women might resist an approach that is less structured and systematic?

2. Barbara shared a time when a third party tried to match her with a younger woman who did not follow through on the meeting. Barbara's feelings could have easily been hurt, discouraging her from future mentoring. How can mentors today learn not to take these situations personally? What enables Barbara to continue including mentoring as part of her life?

3. Some young women are fragile about asking an older woman to meet with them. How can you create an environment that gives them confidence to ask?

4. How does the mentor's new role as guide change your attitude or thoughts about mentoring?

5. How do you feel about turning the responsibility to initiate a mentoring relationship over to the mentee? How might you let a mentee know that you are open to the idea while still putting the ultimate decision on her?

6. What are your thoughts about "multiple mentors"?

Fast Track

1. Ask mentors to read Chapter 4 before the training session.

2. The facilitator briefly reviews the bullet points under **Training Goal**.

3. Discuss questions 1, 4, and 5 under **Group Discussion**.

Training Session Five

A New Commitment: Natural and Organic

Training Goal

The purpose of this training session is to help mentors feel positive and confident when they replace a systematic approach to mentoring with a more natural organic style. For some older women this change may feel like losing control, dumbing down the impact, giving in to an approach that misses the mark. Since they can't measure the outcome as easily, they may sense that they aren't really accomplishing what God wants them to accomplish. We hope this training session will set their minds at ease and remove doubts.

Participant's Home Assignment

Ask mentors to read Chapter 5 and jot down their impressions to aid in the group discussion later.

TRAINING SESSION

Teaching Time

Prepare a brief teaching time to help the concepts in Chapter 5 stick in the minds and hearts of the participants.

Group Discussion

1. How have you seen the idea of "organic" affecting friends, family, or neighbors? How has the organic movement affected you personally?

2. How do you feel about changing from scheduled to more flexible meeting times?

3. Do you think it's possible to be both intentional *and* organic in your mentoring approach?

4. How do you feel about being the one in the relationship who loves first and gives up preferences?

5. How important is motivation in the learning process?

6. Comment on the four different forms of mentoring in the chapter: formal, informal, passive, and group. Which best fits your mentoring style? Share personal experiences you've enjoyed with any of these different mentoring forms.

7. What about an organic mentoring approach appeals to you? What concerns you? How might this kind of mentoring benefit you, the mentor?

Activity

Interview

If you know someone who has adopted an organic approach to life, interview that person. Bring in a gardening or cooking expert, even a midwife from a birthing center, anyone who believes and lives the organic lifestyle. Ask, Why do you like this approach? Specifically how has this approach changed your life? What did you learn that might help you understand why a more organic way of mentoring might work well with young women? Be sure to counsel the mentors not to pass judgment on what they see and hear when their guest is present, but simply use this time as an opportunity to understand this philosophy of life.

Debriefing Question

What did you learn that might help you understand why a more organic way of mentoring might work well with young women?

Fast Track

1. Ask mentors to read Chapter 5 before the session.

2. Discuss questions 2, 4, 6, and 7 under **Group Discussions**.

Training Session Six

A New Goal:
Transformation Through Shared Experiences

Training Goal

This session focuses on the implications of different generational learning styles. The goal is to help mentors understand how attempts to mentor through curriculums may perpetuate the disconnect between generations. In this session mentors learn how to "see" their mentee and help her live as a godly woman in a broken world. This session introduces new mentoring skills: transparency, sharing life stories, mutuality, and intentional listening.

Participant's Home Assignment

Ask mentors to read Chapter 6 and make note of the ways postmodern women prefer to learn. Then ask them to take the "Listening Skills Assessment" on page 200 and bring it to the training session.

Training Session

Discuss the Listening Skills Assessment

Note to leader: To be wise guides, mentors must master the skill of active listening. Most of us are born with the ability to hear, but listening is an acquired skill. Competent listening builds rapport, trust, and meaningful interaction. Because young women long for a wise and patient listener, mentors must learn to be "all ears."

Scoring the Listening Skills Assessment

Listening well involves four basic skills: showing interest, avoiding interruption, mentally organizing information, and postponing evaluation. Odd numbered questions indicate you listen well. Even numbered questions indicate areas where you can improve your listening skills.

Ask mentors what they learned about their listening skills from the

"Listening Skills Assessment." Were any surprised by the results? What do they need to do to become more skilled at listening?

Teaching Time
Ask a speaker to teach on listening skills.

Group Discussion
The Peril of the Pendulum
Display the following paragraph and open it up for discussion:

> *Some Modern women grew up in homes where parents believed too much affirmation would spoil them. As a result, these women struggled to overcome poor self-images and lack confidence. Many of them determined that they would parent differently. They showered their children with encouraging words, making sure that each one felt special and capable of accomplishing whatever he or she dreamed. Now some of these children struggle with entitlement, grandiose expectations, and skewed thinking.*

You could ask questions like, Do you agree or disagree with this paragraph? How can we encourage and affirm our mentees while still preparing them for the real world?

Mentoring with Intentionality
The strongest push back we heard from mentors was the charge that an organic approach to mentoring would result in little or no real mentoring—a valid concern. We hear you. Mentoring is more than hanging out. To drive home this important concept, ask a teacher to distill the points on pages 128–131, or lead a related discussion, whatever you think would work best with your group. How do you adopt an organic approach but include intentionality that's needed to make it happen?

Additional Questions
1. What agendas do modern women commonly bring to mentoring? Why do they like these agendas?

2. Why do you think Postmoderns insist that truth be connected to real-life situations?

3. How comfortable are you with a focus on processing life rather than a prepackaged curriculum? Can you discern why you feel this way?

4. Read the frustrated woman's comments on the lack of transparency among Christians on page 125. Do you agree or disagree? Discuss.

5. How comfortable are you sharing your failures as well as your triumphs? Can you discern why? Discuss appropriate and inappropriate vulnerability.

6. Describe a time when someone's life experience helped you understand an important truth.

7. Think of some ways a mentor can learn from her mentee. How does it change the relationship when both mentor and mentee seek to learn and grow through the connection?

8. Which of the "new" mentoring skills (transparency, sharing of life stories, mutuality, and intentional listening) do you already possess? Which will be difficult for you and why?

9. Discuss these common mentor mistakes and how to avoid them:
   • The mentor's job is to fix the mentee.
   • The mentor is the problem solver.
   • The mentor should produce a woman like herself.
   • The mentor is a wisdom dispenser.
   • The mentee is obligated to accept the mentor's advice.

Activities

Visual Impact

Acquire a copy of *The Joy Luck Club* and play *June's Story,* scene nine, the dialogue between mother Suyuan and daughter June. After viewing the clip, ask participants what emotions bubbled up as they watched? Do they feel "seen" in their own lives? Why is it vital that mentors "see" their mentees? Explain that the purpose of this training session is to teach them how to "see" the women God entrusts to them, so they mentor them with grace, power, and wisdom.

Transparent Storytelling
Pair up and practice telling each other about a difficult time when God worked in your life. For example, you could talk about a time of fear, depression, anxiety, discouragement, pride, jealousy, doubt, failure, or restoration. Include your honest thoughts, feelings, and responses, and how God was present or seemed absent. The woman listening should not talk, but may want to occasionally affirm the speaker. Consider setting a time limit and notifying the women when it's time to switch speakers.

Afterward, in the large group discuss what you learned.

Fast Track

1. Ask mentors to read Chapter 6 and take the "Listening Skills Assessment" before the training session.

2. During the session discuss question 2, 3, and 5 under **Group Discussion**, or carry out the transparent story-telling activity.

To Celebrate
A *Fusion* Gathering

For your last time together, ask potential mentees to join you for a time of mutual insight, celebration, and fun. Work with the younger women to create this gathering, or *Fusion*. Come up with creative ideas that fit your community. Brainstorm how to make this time together meaningful for both mentors and mentees. We have suggested a number of ideas below. Use any of them or come up with your own. When you meet together practice your focused listening skills and all you have learned in the mentor's training. Think of this as your final exam to see if you can put the training concepts into practice!

A gathering like this might serve as a connection point for some organic mentoring in the future, especially if the mentees' training has been coordinated with the mentor's training—both ending in a time of mutual fellowship, prayer, or possibly shared mentoring stories.

Consider providing everyone with **contact information** in case you or a mentor wants to extend an invitation for an outing or coffee together.

Celebration Ideas

Create ways to stick the concepts and memories of what you learned in the minds and hearts of the women who participated. Again, if it's intergenerational, let the younger women invest and participate in the leading. Here are some ideas:

- Give participants a small gift that symbolizes the significance of mentoring
- Enjoy a time of worship to bond your hearts together, choosing music special to both generations
- Create and implement a ceremony to celebrate intergenerational connections
  - » Make rope bracelets that symbolize unity among women regardless of age
  - » Plant flowers together and watch them grow over time to symbolize your growth together through a mutually satisfying relationship
- Enter into a prayer time together to ask the Lord's blessing on future relationships
- Cook and Connect
  - » Cook together wherever the gathering is held. Enjoy eating the food you prepared. Encourage mixed-generation seating.
  - » Discuss prepared questions at each table. For example: When was the first time you fell in love? What's one thing you kept from your parents and never told them? How many technical devices do you own? Where have you traveled? Who were or are the women of your generation to emulate and why?

- Discovery Potluck and People
  - » Ask each woman to bring a potluck dish she prepared. Gather around tables, sit together for a meal, and place the food in the center of the table. Encourage mixed-generation seating. As you enjoy the meal ask each participant to tell why she chose this dish and why she likes it. You could include questions similar to those for the "Cook and Connect" to help everyone get to know one another better.
- Consider a team-building activity where you accomplish a task together
- Enjoy an informal intergenerational movie night together (Watch a film like *Steel Magnolias, The Joy Luck Club,* or *The Secret Life of Bees* and discuss.)

Another Option

If mentors express that they would like to discuss Chapter 8 on Technology in *Organic Mentoring,* you may want to add an additional session. Reading Chapter 8 will not be necessary for women to participate in and enjoy the discussion. Talk about this topic in a large group or circle up in smaller mixed-age groups. Discussing technology with younger women might produce some *Aha!* moments for everyone. Mentees could also spend some time helping mentors understand or hone their technological skills in a practical workshop atmosphere. A little reverse mentoring. If you choose to add a technology component to your time together, here are some discussion questions.

1. What is your attitude toward technology? What do you love about it? Name some benefits of technology.

2. How would you use technology in a mentoring relationship?

3. Compare screen-to-screen relationships with face-to-face relationships. Which are easier for you? What are the downsides and upsides of each?

4. How do you think technology impacts our relationship with God?

AN END AND NEW BEGINNINGS. . .

Will mentors want to continue meeting periodically for additional refresher training times or just to share what they are learning in their mentoring relationships? Do you want to schedule additional *Fusion* gatherings to give older and younger women more time to connect organically? If so, you may want to ask a group of both older and younger women to determine how to make that happen. Remember the tension between keeping the connections natural and organic while still practicing enough intentionality so that opportunities occur. May God bless you in your efforts to love one another and learn together. We would love to hear your stories. Contact us at sedwards@dts.edu or bneumann@dts.edu so we can celebrate with you.

Sue and Barbara

God's richest blessings on you and your new mentoring relationships. May they bless each of you beyond measure and may they glorify the God we all love.

MENTOR'S SELF-ASSESSMENT

Answer the following questions honestly to learn more about your mentoring assumptions and tendencies. Rate yourself on the scale from 1 to 5, with 1 being *never true* and 5 being *absolutely true*.

1	2	3	4	5
(never true)	(seldom true)	(sometimes true)	(usually true)	(absolutely true)

1. A Titus 2 mentoring relationship is one-on-one. _____

2. I prefer that my mentee and I go through a book or do a Bible study together. _____

3. It is appropriate and wise to keep my past mistakes or failures private. _____

4. I prefer to find a mentee through a program that matches us according to interests or other similarities. _____

5. A mentee should respect my authority because I'm older and wiser. _____

6. It is my responsibility to correct my mentee's unwise behavior. _____

7. The Bible teaches specific roles for how we should live as a Christian woman. _____

8. Regular meetings are necessary for a mentoring relationship to thrive. _____

9. My task is to pour wisdom and knowledge into my mentee. _____

10. I expect to meet with my mentee at least once a month. _____

11. A "click" is desirable but not always necessary in a mentoring relationship. _____

12. I expect to set up meetings by phone or email. _____

13. If a mentee does not exhibit commitment, she is not serious about mentoring. _____

14. I expect a mentoring relationship to end after a scheduled term so I can mentor others. _____

15. A book or discipleship curriculum is the best way to teach my mentee biblical truth. _____

16. Familiarity with technology is not important when it comes to mentoring. _____

17. Outside of mentoring, I prefer to learn and grow with people my own age. _____

THE MENTOR'S PERSPECTIVE

Check the statements that are true about you. Try to answer honestly. No one will see this assessment but you.

1. I'm not sure I have enough biblical knowledge or wisdom to be a mentor. _____

2. My lack of formal education disqualifies me to mentor younger, more educated women. _____

3. I'm not sure I have enough time in my schedule to be a mentor. _____

4. I have too many failures in my life to effectively mentor another woman. _____

5. I served in the church for many years and now it's someone else's turn. _____

6. If I say yes to mentoring, I'm afraid I'll never be able to get out of it. _____

7. I'm afraid I won't know what to say to a mentee, so I shouldn't commit. _____

8. I can't relate to the younger generations; I simply don't understand them. _____

9. I'm afraid a mentee will need more than I can give. _____

10. I have enough problems of my own; I can't take on someone else's. _____

11. I travel too much and since mentoring requires regular meetings, I can't be a mentor. _____

LISTENING SKILLS ASSESSMENT

Check the statements that describe you.

1. When my mentee is speaking, I look at her, lean forward slightly, and occasionally nod my head. _____

2. If I disagree with my mentee, I feel it's important to offer my perspective as she is speaking. _____

3. I listen in order to learn what I don't know about my mentee and her situation. _____

4. I can quickly discern if my mentee is on the wrong track. _____

5. I can block out distractions taking place around us. _____

6. Sometimes my mind wanders when she is speaking. _____

7. I will often say, "Tell me more about that," or "What did you mean by. . . ?" _____

8. If I don't approve of something she said, I instinctively frown or knit my eyebrows. _____

9. I can remember her main points and periodically paraphrase what she has said. _____

10. I often multitask while listening—check my phone, finish a chore, send a text, speak to a child. _____

11. I pick up on the feelings behind my mentee's words. _____

12. I talk as much as my mentee, sometimes more. _____

13. I wait for her to finish speaking and pause briefly before I respond. _____

14. While she is speaking I think about what I will say next. _____

15. She often says to me, "Thanks for listening." _____

16. I sometime fidget (tap my fingers, chew on a pen, shake my leg) while listening. _____

17. I refrain from making any judgments about her situation until she has finished talking. _____

18. People often think I am too busy to talk to them. _____

19. I listen for God's movement in my mentee's life. _____

APPENDIX B

NextGen Preps

A Note to Mentees from Authors Sue and Barbara:

We wrote *Organic Mentoring* to help women our age change outdated approaches so that we might be more effective as your mentors. We were mentored years ago by your grandmothers before the earth's crust cooled. No, not that far back, but far enough back that you would hardly recognize that world. We are Moderns, the last generation of the modern era. You are Postmoderns, the first generation of a new era. A wide chasm divides us, and yet we love you dearly and want to journey with you through this ever-changing world. Christ has called us to care about you and walk beside you—if you want us to. But it's hard for many of us. We grew up with different ways of thinking and living, and we are trying to adjust. We need your grace and patience.

Our book speaks specifically to older women, our peers, but we hope that you will find parts of our book useful in creating mentoring relationships that work for you. Stats tell us that most of you are wide open to mentoring, but that many of you have been disappointed in the programmatic mentoring typical in many places today. We hope to change that. We're both seminary professors who specialize in ministries with women. We've both mentored women all our lives and care deeply about your generation. Barbara did her doctoral dissertation on reasons why many mentoring relationships aren't working for younger women today. Sue was her advising professor on the project. The result is our book, *Organic Mentoring*.

Worn-Out Mentoring Models

We are experiencing a mentoring crisis today. Many of you seek mentors

203

but find few willing older women. The result—too many in your generation struggle to figure out the Christian life on their own. We find the answer to our mentoring crisis in God's Word. After leading the Israelites out of slavery in Egypt and into the Promised Land, Moses wrote,

> Love the LORD your God with all your heart and with all your soul and with all your strength. These commandments that I give you today are to be on your hearts. Impress them on your children. Talk about them when you sit at home and when you walk along the road, when you lie down and when you get up. Deuteronomy 6:5–7

Moses first wrote these words for parents to help them pass on their faith to their children, but they apply equally well to mentoring. Moses instructs mentors to "impress" (*Shanan*) our love for God on you, but to do so in a natural kind of way. The Hebrew word for "impress" means to whet your appetites for God, to sharpen you spiritually. He tells us to mentor *when you sit at home and when you walk along the road, when you lie down and when you get up*. These verses ooze a casual, natural informality.

Moses asked parents to speak of their love for God in those natural everyday moments of life, sitting together at home, walking from place to place, to take advantage of teachable times when questions naturally arise. We apply this concept to mentoring when our relationships take on an informal feel, simply doing life together. We call this new approach to mentoring *organic*. What a surprise to find our answer to the mentoring crisis in ancient biblical wisdom.

A New Approach Deserves a New Label

The word *mentoring* conjures up so many stereotypes and hang-ups that we prefer to stop using it or any formal word for the relationship. That's a more organic approach and may help us all rid ourselves of expectations that tend to discourage us from "mentoring" relationships anyway.

We enjoy sweet relationships with a number of women in our seminary and in our churches, but the relationships seldom begin with a formal invitation like, "Will you be my mentor?" It just happens. We will use the terms *mentoring, mentor,* and *mentee* in this NextGen Prep because we need to call it something. But we encourage everyone to move away from formal terms as a first step in adopting a new mentoring mind-set.

About This Resource

This resource contains two sessions designed to prepare young women to understand older women and to help you understand how to do your part to make organic mentoring relationships work well. You might use it to educate yourself and your peers so that you are ready and equipped to partner with older women in significant mentoring relationships. (If you are an older woman who wants to offer training to mentees in conjunction with training for mentors [Appendix A], we suggest that you identify several younger women to lead this training with you or for you. You may want to delegate the whole training process to them.)

Your Part

To help prepare for your part in mentoring, we ask you to join once or twice with other young women interested in quality relationships with older women. Ideally, meet in an informal setting like a coffee shop or living room. The material is designed around a discussion format, although the participants will be asked to read some valuable information as a basis for the discussion. We recommend you meet together with other younger women twice, but if that's not feasible, we've provided a Fast Track, making this doable in one gathering.

We've planned an optional final session where younger and older women meet together. Its purpose is to jump-start organic mentoring connections in your community. Feel free to tweak or combine training sessions to suit your group. Make the material work for you. A helpful suggestion: schedule your meetings so they conclude at the same time the mentor training concludes.

We ask you to read Chapter 3 in *Organic Mentoring*, a chapter that should help you understand older women. As you read, remember the chapter was not written to you, but to your mentor. Think of yourself as peering over her shoulder as she learns more about you, herself, and new approaches that we hope will work well for you both. Or maybe as a fly on the wall. The end game, in our minds and hearts, is to foster the kinds of relationships that provide you with loving, insightful guides who understand you, see you, and help you navigate the crazy world you live in. Jesus modeled these kinds of relationships for us. Paul mandated that we are responsible to provide you with the kind of care and direction that will help you thrive and grow strong, joyful, and fulfilled in your Christian life. In our book, we challenge mentors to make major changes in their mentoring approaches, but they will need your help. These sessions were created to help you help us. So dig in and learn all you can. Our fervent prayer is that you'll receive far more than you invest.

FIRST PREP
UNDERSTANDING YOUR MENTORS

To Get Ready:
Read Chapter 3 of *Organic Mentoring*. This chapter describes characteristics typical of many older women, and explains why they tend to favor traditional mentoring methods.

Discuss your thoughts in response to Chapter 3.

Possible Questions:
1. Examine the list of modern values carefully. How do these typical qualities help you understand older women you know?

2. What modern values cause older women to mentor in ways that don't work for you? Does understanding these values help you exhibit more patience with older women?

3. What modern women's values and challenges make mentoring difficult or scary for her?

4. Have you ever felt that older women weren't interested in mentoring you? Can you share an experience when you were hurt or discouraged by her actions or attitude?

5. How might you exhibit grace and patience when you observe a mentor wrestling with these issues?

Going Further Ideas

1. You might invite several older women to join you, share their stories, and respond to your questions. After they leave, talk together about what you learned.

2. Use your creativity. Get into smaller groups and create a collage that represents your generation and your parents' generation. Provide a large poster board for each group and magazines, online articles, colored paper, markers, scissors, glue, etc. Divide the poster equally to represent Moderns and Postmoderns, possibly front and back. After everyone is finished, ask groups to explain their posters.

SECOND PREP

YOU INITIATE THE MATCH AND DRIVE THE RELATIONSHIP

This book recommends an organic approach that allows mentoring to flow from natural life relationships and events. Instead of a pairing program, young women find their own mentors based on natural attraction and mentoring needs. The focus of the relationship switches from the mentor's wisdom to the mentee's spiritual journey. The younger woman drives the relationship and the mentor comes alongside as a trusted guide. Schedules and curriculums are set aside, and mentor and mentee meet as questions or needs arise in the process of doing life.

To Get Ready

Gather a group of young women to discuss your responsibilities in an organic approach. Appoint a facilitator to guide the discussion.

Possible Discussion Questions

Read the following excerpts from the book and discuss.

Mentee Selects Her Mentor

From our research and experience, we believe that older women must graciously release the mentor selection process and place it in the hands of the young women. They must be free to choose their own mentors.

The relationship needs to be comfortable from the beginning. The starting point for most next generation women is trust. The trustworthy character of a potential mentor is more important to young women than whatever else the two women might have in common. A relationship of knowing, even if it is just observation from a distance, is necessary *before* a match. Although older women can still initiate, young women become the driving force behind mentor selection. Lindsey, age 25, says, "I'm a firm believer that it's the mentee's job to find her mentor. I hate that it has come to where it has to be matched. That is just so unnatural."

1. Can you describe a time you were drawn to or identified a potential mentor on your own?

2. What elements would make a mentoring match "click" for you?

Mentee Takes the Initiative

Now that the selection process is turned around and the mentee is free to select a mentor according to her needs, how does she connect with a mentor? In addition to prayer, we believe a young woman will move toward a mentor based on her personal needs and life circumstances. Natural attraction helps her find the right person at the right time.

An organic mentoring relationship typically starts with an informal invitation to meet, usually initiated by the younger woman. "I was wondering if you could meet me for coffee? I would love your input on a situation." The invitation is as simple as that. Over coffee the two women can discern if there is a click and if they want to meet again.

Although it's a simple act, the way a mentee approaches us makes a difference. If she asks, "Will you be my mentor?" or "Will you mentor me?"she may unknowingly put us in an awkward position, and she may get a deer-in-the-headlights response. Our minds immediately envision endless meetings, pouring out wisdom we don't have, responsibility for another's spiritual development, and lots of time. Our brains frantically send out preserve-your-life signals, so we politely decline and assure the young woman that it's nothing personal. The phrase "Will you be my mentor?" can burden an invitation with expectations that scare many of us off, but we find an invitation for coffee easy to accept. We believe older women are more receptive if young women avoid the word *mentor*.

Some young women may lack the confidence to initiate a mentoring relationship, even to invite an older woman to a simple coffee outing. For them, the possibility of rejection isn't worth the risk, so they continue their lonely walk, without the guidance they yearn for.

Finding healthy mentoring relationships, for both mentor and mentee, resembles a dance. Each one takes steps toward or away from the other, as each discerns if this match is God's idea. Ultimately, the mentee must take the lead, even if she's shy and awkward. The relationship must meet the needs in *her* life, although the mentor can influence that decision, much like a responsive dance partner.

1. An organic mentoring relationship is about you, and you must ultimately make choices that work for you. This requires you to take the initiative.
   - How do you feel about this responsibility?
   - What hinders you?
   - What might help you take this step?
   - How could a potential mentor make you feel more comfortable taking the initiative?

Mentee Drives the Relationship

In the past we made mentoring about the mentor. The mentoring spotlight focused on her wisdom, talent, and godly behavior. If we look at mentoring as a stage play, the mentor would traditionally be cast in the starring role. The mentee was the understudy, a less experienced actress with a small part. She sat at the mentor's feet to learn her ways.

An organic approach swings the spotlight from mentor to mentee. The mentor steps out of the spotlight and places the mentee in the primary role. The mentee's life situation and learning needs drive the relationship. This shift in emphasis changes the ethos of the relationship, which becomes more like a greenhouse focused on the one who needs care and tending.

Instead of occupying an elevated place where she pours out knowledge, the mentor comes alongside to guide, counsel, encourage, and support the mentee as she learns to journey with Christ. Times of instruction, guidance, and wisdom will certainly be a part of this process, but mentoring is primarily about the needs, goals, and desires of the one being mentored.

1. If the mentor functions in the role of guide, what might happen if you have no idea where you want to go or what you want to learn with her? How could your lack of clarity make the situation awkward for the mentor?

2. An organic approach often requires some intentionality to make mentoring actually happen. Brainstorm ideas to help create organic mentoring situations that would work for you.

Fast Track:

Instead of two meetings, combine both **Preps** into one meeting. Although it takes some time, we feel it's important that young women read all of Chapter 3. This chapter describes your mentors and is key to understanding how to relate to them well. Discuss questions 2, 6, and 7 under **First Prep**.

As time allows, read and discuss the questions under **Second Prep**. Be sure potential mentees know their responsibilities include initial contact with the mentor of their choice and driving the relationship.

A *FUSION* GATHERING

For an additional time together, ask potential mentors to join you for a time of mutual insight, celebration, and fun. Work with the older women to create this gathering. In light of what you've learned, think of additional questions you want to ask or ideas you want to convey that might help them.

A gathering like this might serve as a connection point for some organic mentoring in the future, especially if your training has been coordinated with the mentors' training—both ending in a time of mutual fellowship, prayer, or possibly shared mentoring stories.

For this mutual gathering, or *Fusion*, come up with creative ideas that fit your context. Be sure to work with the older women and, when you meet together, practice being direct and kind in expressing your views on what you would like to see happen.

At the gathering, be sure to provide everyone with contact information in case you or a mentor wants to extend an invitation for an outing or coffee together.

An End and a New Beginning. . .

Here are some ideas for a *Fusion* event:

- Give participants a small gift that symbolizes the significance of mentoring
- Enjoy a time of worship to bond your hearts together, choosing music special to both generations
- Create and implement a ceremony to celebrate intergenerational connections
- Enter into a prayer time together to ask the Lord's blessing on future relationships
- Cook and Connect
  - » Cook together wherever the gathering is held. Enjoy eating the food you prepared. Encourage mixed-generation seating.
  - » Discuss prepared questions at each table. For example: When was the first time you fell in love? What's one thing you kept from your parents and never told them? How many technical devices do you own? Where have you traveled? Who were or are the women of your generation to emulate and why?
- Discovery Potluck and People
  - » Ask each woman to bring a potluck dish she prepared. Gather around tables, sit together for a meal, and place the food in the center of the table. Encourage mixed-generation seating. As you enjoy the meal ask each participant to tell why she chose this dish and why she likes it. You could include questions similar to those for the "Cook and Connect" to help everyone get to know one another better. You could also discuss how technology might affect a mentoring relationship today.

- Consider a team building activity where you accomplish a task together
- Enjoy an informal intergenerational movie night together (Watch a film like *Steel Magnolias, The Joy Luck Club,* or *The Secret Life of Bees* and discuss.)

God's richest blessings on you and your new mentoring relationships. May they inspire and encourage each of you beyond measure and may they glorify the God we all love.

APPENDIX C

A Leader's Guide to Start and Maintain a Mentoring Culture

WHERE TO START?

So here you are, a leader motivated to create a mentoring culture in your church or community. You are convinced mentoring programs with matchmakers, predetermined schedules, and curriculums belong to a past era. You grasp ways young women are different from you. You are alert to the mentoring crisis we face. You may also wonder, *What do I do now? How does an organic mentoring process start from scratch?* We offer a few practical suggestions for those who need help getting started.

Remember, mentoring today requires an organic feel or postmodern women will stay away. At the same time, some intentional groundwork may be helpful for organic mentoring to work well. We found that a purely organic process without intentionality seldom secures the desired results. If you want to facilitate organic mentoring relationships, you will need to create just enough underlying structure to encourage the process, but without a structured feel.

Start with a Team

Organic mentoring grows in the rich soil of community. Start your mentoring initiative by recruiting a multigenerational team of women passionate about mentoring. To gain the confidence of postmodern women, include young women on this team. As these women work together their unity, energy, and relationships will model community for other women.

Some of the women could serve in different functions on this team. Consider these possibilities:

- Team Leader—this woman oversees the process.
- Trainer/Equipper—this woman organizes training opportunities for both mentors and mentees.
- Mentoring Consultant—this woman is a resource for those who need help getting started. She knows potential mentors and mentees and can assist those who are not sure how to make a mentoring connection. She doesn't match, but suggests possibilities for a mentee or mentor to investigate.
- Shepherd to the Mentors—this woman cares for and encourages the mentors. She keeps up with them, knows what obstacles they face, and lets them know they are valuable. She may want to arrange periodic lunches/dinners to allow mentors to share experiences, problems, solutions, ideas, etc. Through her care, mentors feel connected and supported instead of out there on their own. She can also be a confidential resource for women experiencing "issues" in their relationships.
- Creative Input—this woman (or women) keeps fresh ideas before the team.

A dynamic team lays the groundwork for organic mentoring. They also pray for the process and the women involved. Prayer is an essential pillar in the infrastructure, and one important reason to create a team.

Follow with Focus Groups

You might gather a diverse group of young women and ask them for their thoughts on mentoring. What ideas do they have? What won't work for them? What does their typical week look like? What challenges do they face? How are their lives different? What help do they want from a mentor? Listen carefully to their responses. Take note of common themes, concerns, desires, and preferences. Each community of young women will be different. Learn about yours. These focus groups offer guidance for the way forward.

Develop a Plan

Take what you learn from your young women and this book and develop a plan to create mentoring opportunities in your community. The plan should specifically reflect the preferences of your young women. A range of options creates a more organic feel.

Provide Training

We provide training materials for mentors in Appendix A. Training designed specifically for modern women will help them adjust to postmodern ways. As you meet, gently motivate Moderns to let go of outdated methods and embrace approaches that lead to more successful relationships today. Acquaint mentors with the new possibilities and how they work. Be sure to emphasize that these new methods are beneficial for both generations. We believe that because older mentors are the ones who must make major adjustments, they need the most preparation.

Younger women need to recognize that responsibility to initiate and drive mentoring relationships has shifted to them. Unless they play an active part, the relationship probably won't thrive. Training will help them understand their biblical obligation to learn from mature believers. Also help them understand that cooperative, generous attitudes will open mentoring doors for them.

Most postmodern women already approach life with an organic mindset, so their training needs will be minimal. Appendix B is designed to help mentees understand their older mentors and make the most of organic opportunities. Or you may want to create your own materials. In an established mentoring culture, the young women will clue in their newcomer friends and mentee training may not be necessary at all.

When adapting to new methods, training helps everyone feel secure and find their way. With proper preparation, all the women understand their part in the new approach, resulting in fewer disgruntled participants. Take the time to train well.

Connect the Women

If your community tends to be age segregated, you may need to start with bridge events. A bridge event is designed to introduce the generations to each other and give them an opportunity to connect. Women get acquainted over a meal, activity, or outing. At some point during the event, ask a potential mentor to transparently share something about her personal faith journey. At one such event a deeply respected older woman, a former missionary, began her talk this way, "Hello. My name is Isabel and I am a recovering deceitful, spiteful, perfectionistic, scared, lonely, and unforgiving woman." She went on to relate personal experiences of subsequent transformation through her faith in Jesus. She didn't hide the rough years. Young women all over the room hung on every word. When she finished they swarmed around her, eager to know her better.

Young women get to know potential mentors when mentors share their stories. This first step in organic pairing provides opportunities for young women to learn more about older women, enabling them to discover potential "clicks."

Segregated communities may also benefit from additional sources of information. With mentors' permission, you could provide a website and/or hard copies that include a mentor's biographical information, pictures, and a few personal tidbits as a way to help young women discern a potential click. This would be a great project for a group of younger tech-savvy women.

If your mentoring community is large, you may need to identify women willing to mentor. They might wear a small but distinctive tag on their clothing or some other ornament to let young women know they are available to mentor. This way a young woman can quietly observe or casually converse with a potential mentor to see if there is a natural connection. Once organic mentoring is established, you may choose to eliminate these aids, or you might find they are part of the necessary groundwork that helps your women connect.

Keep It Simple

The above suggestions are intended to help you consider what type of underlying structure you might need to get started. The infrastructure should be mostly invisible to young women. They should feel their mentoring connections happen naturally. You and a few others know that some organization was required to create that natural opportunity, but it barely shows. You may find some or all of this structure can even be dropped when an organic culture is successfully established.

Don't Rush

Change takes time and energy. Resist the pressure to set an artificial start date . . . say, by September 1st. Organic processes roll out without fanfare or announcements. They simply are. When you sense that older women are on board and well trained, release them and let the Holy Spirit ordain relationships naturally, as younger women take the initiative.

MAINTAINING THE ORGANIC CULTURE

An organic mentoring culture remains strong as long as church leaders and older women value mentoring as a key opportunity to grow women. When mentoring young women becomes embedded in the attitudes and practices of the wider community, organic mentoring thrives. Here are a few ideas to maintain robust mentoring.

Keep the vision strong. If the vision grows dim, so do opportunities. From time to time a leader might speak about the biblical mandate to pass on Christian faith, as well as the benefits of mentoring. Keep the Deuteronomy 6 passage fresh in women's hearts.

Take care of your mentors. If mentoring is truly organic, not every mentor will be obvious or even known. Often, a core of mentors can be identified and offered support. Mentors do get tired, doubt their effectiveness, or sometimes have bad experiences. Encouragement and support helps retain their participation.

Facilitate intergenerational community. Organic mentoring relationships germinate when women of all ages know each other. We find the greatest obstacle to organic mentoring is age segregation. Continue to keep your women connected.

Evaluate regularly. Organic mentoring is a living organism that takes on a life of its own. When we lift the artificial ropes, we never know exactly what we will get. Evaluation is challenging when mentoring relationships are no longer official events, but it is still essential to check the health of the relationships. Focus groups can be helpful in evaluating organic mentoring. Periodically gather a group of young women and ask them for feedback. How do they believe it's going? Are there problems? What would they suggest? Do the same with a group of older women. By it's nature, an organic environment will move and change; prepare to make adjustments as you go. Be sure to communicate the results of your evaluation to the women involved.

Provide periodic equipping. As new women become interested in mentoring, you may want to offer training again.